C000005569

Talent o

Getting the best from freelancers, interims and consultants

Emma Brierley founded her own freelance resourcing agency Xchangeteam in 1999 and now acts as CEO. She has had 10 years' background in the industry working for a number of PR agencies, and then four years as a freelance public relations consultant. Emma writes and speaks regularly about freelance issues, HR and recruitment trends.

The Chartered Institute of Personnel and Development is the leading publisher of books and reports for personnel and training professionals, students, and all those concerned with the effective management and development of people at work. For details of all our titles, please contact the Publishing Department:

tel. 020-8612 6204
e-mail publish@cipd.co.uk
The catalogue of all CIPD titles can be viewed on the CIPD website:
www.cipd.co.uk/bookstore

Talent on Tap

Getting the best from freelancers, interims and consultants

Emma Brierley

Chartered Institute of Personnel and Development

Published by the Chartered Institute of Personnel and Development,
151 The Broadway, London, SW19 1JQ

First published 2006

Typeset by Fakenham Photosetting, Fakenham, Norfolk

Printed in Great Britain by Cromwell Press, Trowbridge, Wiltshire

British Library Cataloguing in Publication Data
A catalogue of this publication is available from the British Library

ISBN 1 84398 140 8
ISBN-13 978 1 84398 140 4

Chartered Institute of Personnel and Development
151 The Broadway, Wimbledon, London SW19 1JQ
Tel: 020-8612 6200
E-mail: cipd@cipd.co.uk Website: www.cipd.co.uk
Incorporated by Royal Charter. Registered Charity No. 1079797.

Contents

List of Figures

List of Tables

Acknowledgements

This book might have remained a twinkle in my eye without the encouragement, support and insight of a large group of people. At the risk of sounding like a recipient at the Oscars, I would like to thank Charles Handy, Bill Noon, John Knell and Simon Juden for their intellectual insight; Kerry Potter, Kelly Partridge and the team of agents at Xchangeteam for their expert input and coordination; the numerous contributors who shared their personal experiences; and, of course, the wider freelance community, without whom there would be no need for this book.

Foreword

One UK worker in seven chooses to work for himself or herself, rather than for any fixed employer. Some are 'temps', and some have taken a career decision to operate freelance long-term. There are an estimated 1 million people in this latter category. They include many of the country's most experienced and knowledgeable workers, and this highly skilled, highly mobile and highly flexible twenty-first-century workforce is growing – a trend that is likely to continue.

The UK's freelancing model is unique in the developed world and represents one of the country's greatest economic assets. Derek Wreay, former Chair of the Association of Technology Staffing Companies, says:

> *A vibrant, highly skilled and committed freelance workforce is one of the cornerstones of UK plc's success. It is an area in which the UK leads in Europe, and this is a tribute to the competence of our freelancing community, and to the firms whose far-sightedness allows them to benefit from these freelancers' world-class skills.*

Freelancers are not looking for employers to whom they can belong, but networks in which they can thrive. Successful freelancers are trusted advisers with sought-after knowledge, capable of moving quickly between jobs and assignments, transferring ideas, skills and positive attitudes. Freelancers live or die by their reputations, and good freelancers invariably have an extended network of well-known contacts that they can call upon to provide services outside their scope. The value of this to their clients can be immense. Freelancing has now become the preferred way of working, for the very best talent in virtually all sectors.

Without a legal definition, freelancers inhabit the gap between external suppliers and employees. In the UK and the EU, governments have sought to deal with this by legislating that freelancers are more closely aligned with traditional employees. This approach ignores the fact that most freelancers have turned their backs on traditional employment models. Most freelancers do not wish to be viewed as employees or 'temps', nor do they hanker after the benefits and trappings of employment.

Large corporations discovered the benefits of engaging freelance contractors for specific projects a long time ago. Using freelancers to complement the permanent workforce allows flexibility, so that businesses can manage fluctuating demand and take advantage of rapid, low-cost hiring or obligation-free downsizing, as appropriate. By definition, a freelancer is likely to have worked for far more clients than an 'equivalent' employee, and permanent staff within an organisation can benefit enormously from the knowledge transfer and best practice that freelancers bring with them.

Small and medium-sized companies are in an ideal position to take advantage of the many skills and services offered by freelancers, allowing their businesses to be agile and versatile in an increasingly competitive world, as well as leveraging the extensive industry contacts freelancers build up over a career. As the burdens of employment legislation, which weigh disproportionately on the smaller business, become heavier, freelancing offers a pragmatic and flexible resourcing model able to cover specific projects, help cope with peaks in demand and provide valuable advice and expertise.

Making a strategic decision to deploy freelance talent gives businesses flexible access to high-calibre professionals. Compared to larger, more traditional consultancies, freelancers offer excellent value for money, as well as a welcome focus on understanding and working in the client's business, rather than merely executing their own internal processes. An independent freelancer is only ever as good as his or her last assignment, and this motivation is a real driver for quality. When meeting project deadlines is of paramount importance, engaging freelancers can make the difference between success and failure. They usually have the experience, knowledge and expertise to be able to contribute and add value from the outset, and are free to focus solely on the task in hand, without being distracted by internal political considerations.

Headcount considerations aside, freelancers can offer a cost-effective deployment solution, without the usual overheads to support or the burden of employment costs and responsibilities. Many operate from their own premises or homes, attending client sites only when necessary. Freelancers are project-focused, charging only for the time it takes or for performance of the agreed project. They generally charge hourly or daily rates based upon their skills, experience and expertise and take care of their own tax and NI payments, pensions, holiday pay and the like.

Organisations wanting to take advantage of the flexibility, expertise and knowledge that freelancers offer need to understand some basic employment status and tax issues that influence contractual matters. Recent court cases serve to emphasise the risk of a relationship initially viewed as one of self-employment by all parties later being deemed to be one of employment, with the concomitant rights and costs issues. To avoid these risks it is imperative that freelancers are engaged on the right terms and conditions; a chapter in this book deals with these issues in some detail, but broadly where the relationship is one of self-employment, a business-to-business 'contract for service', rather than an employment-style 'contract of service' should be used to protect all parties.

The freelance market has grown considerably in recent years and studies suggest that this trend is set to continue. This book is full of practical, pragmatic advice and guidance, and in my view represents an invaluable addition to the hirer's arsenal, providing clear and useful insights into areas which may be unfamiliar or have changed recently, as well as reference information for those experienced in dealing with the freelance workforce.

Simon Juden
Professional Contractors Group,
the representative body for the
UK's freelance small business community

Preface

I joined the freelance revolution in 1995 – turning my back on a steady PR agency job and opting for the freedom and flexibility of a freelance career – and I have never looked back.

My personal experience of freelancing is overwhelmingly positive. It suited my personality – I loved not knowing what was around the corner, meeting new challenges, working with different people, learning new skills. I found that the lack of political baggage increased my objectivity and meant that I could 'sort through the woods and the trees' to arrive at good counsel. Suddenly I wasn't pigeon-holed into what my employer wanted me to be but could define myself, create my own brand, develop in different directions according to my interests and abilities as well as, of course, to the ever-dominant market.

There was insecurity but you simply had to believe in yourself. If you didn't, then freelancing was unlikely to be the career for you. On the whole I earned more money – but this was only part of the reason I chose to work in this way. Far more important was the increased satisfaction I derived from being in control of my own destiny. It sounds grand, but it is a fundamental issue that goes to the heart of what drives us all.

At length, my freelance experience turned into a full-time vocation. In 1999 I founded Xchangeteam, a specialist freelance resourcing company in marketing and creative services. Essentially, Xchangeteam acts as a broker, matching freelance consultants to business needs. The company is at the heart of the freelance phenomenon, and I have therefore been able to observe both good and bad practices.

One thing that is very apparent is the lack of understanding among hiring organisations of how to get the best from freelance consultants. There can be the expectation that freelance consultants should be totally self-sufficient and require no direction at all. Attitudes can range from 'I am too busy to brief them properly' or 'They are the experts – they don't need any input from me' to 'I'm paying them enough, so they can just get on with it.' Without doubt, poor briefing and objective-setting accounts for the majority of freelance assignment failures. Because companies often bring freelancers in during times of corporate pressure, there can be the tendency not to plan but to be reactive – ad hoc rather than strategic. Many times we have seen poor communication undermine relationships: poor communication between hirer and freelancer and between freelancer and permanent members of staff. Often problems arise as hirers don't understand how a freelance consultant differs from an employee and that the techniques in motivation and performance management must differ.

Frustrated by the lag in professionalism – and well placed as poacher-turned-gamekeeper – I have written *Talent on Tap: Getting the best from freelancers, interims and consultants* as a guide offering practical steps to help hiring organisations plan for and maximise their investment in freelance consultants. It is not rocket science, and as in all good things it is governed by common sense. Ultimately, the key message is that time spent up front setting the relationship and management framework will produce huge dividends later. If you recognise the benefits of using freelancers, then your organisation needs to embrace some of the concepts in the book to create a freelance-friendly culture.

And of course, in the true freelance tradition, I have worked on this book with an expert freelance copywriter, Patrick McKenna, who has helped to craft my and other contributors' ideas and thoughts into an intelligible whole, for which I am very grateful.

My hope is that you will find some practical assistance in this book, which will help you to unlock the huge potential of using a flexible workforce. The dream is that freelancing is a planned part of your HR strategy and enables you to meet the demanding needs of today's global economy by having 'talent on tap'!

Emma Brierley
Xchangeteam Group Limited

Introduction

If freelancers, interims and consultants are not already indispensable to the global economy, they soon will be. Combined with other non-permanent workers, they make up the fastest growing cluster in today's labour market. Currently, they comprise 13 per cent of the UK's workforce: a total of 3.6 million people. It is clear that organisations should be considering the benefits of factoring them into their long-term human resource strategy.

Especially in the UK.

This country has the largest recruitment market in Europe. More than half of all non-permanent positions are filled here. Current figures from the Recruitment and Employment Confederation (REC) indicate that UK organisations are already spending around £22.81 billion annually on non-permanent workers. And according to Key Note this figure is likely to grow to around £25.6 billion by 2009 – a rise of 8 per cent.

These figures raise fundamental questions. How wisely are these billions being invested? How should freelance consultants be managed? How do hiring organisations measure a freelance consultant's performance or assess how much value they add? What risks do they bring and take with them? Are there proven processes to determine their impact on permanent staff? What influence do freelance consultants have on an organisation's internal culture? Inevitably, the answers tend to be as hit-and-miss as the methods currently used to meet the challenges that the freelance option presents.

The absence of a coherent response would not be tolerated in any other part of a properly managed organisation. Yet a lack of management control persists when it comes to freelance consultants – despite the fact that freelance consultants are becoming such an important part of the labour market.

Placing the resurgence of the freelance community in its historical perspective is important to developing new ways to manage it. Until the Industrial Revolution, freelance workers made up the biggest proportion of the working population. It was only when the means of production became too big, expensive and labour-intensive for individuals to manage alone that large organisations took control of the labour market. Gradually, full-time salaried employees became the rule rather than the exception, and the concept of lifelong loyalty in return for a lifetime of job security was born.

Fast-forward to the late twentieth century and the dawn of the Information Revolution, when increasingly affordable and powerful communications technology began moving the means of production back towards the individual. This shift is leaving a growing number of organisations on the wrong side of the employer–employee equation. Now, the history of the freelance worker is coming full-circle and a range of socio-political and economic factors continues to drive the freelance worker's renaissance.

We discuss these drivers in greater detail during the forthcoming chapters. But for now, some food for thought.

Information technology is becoming even more sophisticated and cheaper. Among other changes, this is speeding the pace of globalisation and use of remote working. Meanwhile, workplace demographics are in a state of flux. Few organisations can provide jobs for life while fewer people are prepared to accept the traditional hierarchies that come with them. Men and women are seeking new ways to strike a more equitable work–life balance. Certainly, more women are shaping their personal lives around personal commitments and not vice versa. The proportion of older workers is rising and their experience is becoming more valuable. The skills shortage is intensifying as talent becomes more elusive. Yet the pressure to cut costs and raise profits remains as relentless as ever.

As knowledge overtakes capital and equipment as an organisation's core asset, the most talented and accomplished individuals are discovering that they can sell their expertise where and when they choose – and name their price along the way.

It is against this backdrop that organisations need to start factoring freelance consultants into their long-term strategies. This is why the arguments for and against using freelance consultants must advance beyond the day-to-day minutiae of hourly rates and weekly expense claims towards a more complex debate covering cost benefits, value measurement, knowledge management and corporate cohesion.

It is worth reflecting on the different speeds at which organisations have responded to the freelance challenge. Clearly, those organisations that are ahead of the curve tend to operate in sectors where knowledge has long been the critical source of competitive advantage. The IT sector provides numerous good examples. As the knowledge-based economy continues to expand, organisations across a wider range of sectors are facing up to the freelance challenge for the first time.

As a result of our research, we have based this book on two premises:

- *Premise one*
  To manage freelance consultants effectively, organisations require practical and pragmatic guidance on areas such as cost management, assessing value, selection, contracts, deployment, performance measurement, possible problems, integration, remuneration, termination and relationship-building.

- *Premise two*
  This book does not set out to analyse a fragile and passing trend. It is a response to an irreducible fact of working life: the freelance workforce is back to stay.

1

What is a freelance consultant?

INTRODUCTION

As its title suggests, this book is primarily concerned with how to get the best from three groups of independent workers: freelance consultants, interims and consultants. Together, the Professional Contractors Group (PCG) estimates that they make up around 1 million of the UK workforce.

Why have we chosen to focus on this group? Because they are professionals who have the skills and experience to add significant value to an organisation – provided the organisation understands how to unlock their full potential.

What's in a name?

The terms used to define non-permanent workers are multiplying as rapidly as the flexible working practices they are pioneering. Some terms have been part of the language for a matter of months, others for centuries. Some terms provoke positive reactions, but a surprising number provoke negative reactions. Indeed, we were surprised to find that the semantics of non-permanent working can be highly emotive.

'Temp' is a term that is commonly but not exclusively used to describe office-based support and administration workers, some of them highly skilled – such as PAs. Unfairly, though, the term has developed potentially negative associations, seldom evoking the image of highly skilled and motivated individuals selling their skills at premium rates on their own terms.

'Homeworkers' are widely assumed to be the domestic equivalent of the office temp. Again, this perception is only partly true and ignores the long, colourful and occasionally militant history of homeworkers. In 1877, for example, New York's cigar-makers – mainly female homeworkers from immigrant communities – created a permanent place for themselves in US labour history when they challenged their hirers with a strike.

'Teleworker' and 'telecommuter' are terms that evoke a far more positive up-to-date image. Given their contemporary relevance, it is somewhat surprising to discover that both terms were coined as far back as in 1973 by the American academic, author and futurologist Jack Nilles.

'Teleworking' refers to jobs that use information technology. 'Telecommuting' aims to shorten or eliminate the daily journey to work by using information technology to send work to people, not vice versa.

In his book *The Age of Unreason* (Arrow Business Books, 1989), Charles Handy coined the term 'portfolio worker' to describe an emerging breed of people who hold multiple jobs or contracts in multiple fields with multiple clients and companies.

Twelve years later US author Daniel H. Pink published *Free Agent Nation – The future of working for yourself* (Warner Business Books, 2001). 'Free agent', he explains, is a catch-all term used to describe people who are abandoning one of the Industrial Revolution's most enduring legacies – the job – to become

> **knowledge workers, temps** and **permatemps, freelancers** and **e-lancers, independent contractors** and **independent professionals, micropreneurs** and **infopreneurs, part-time consultants** and **interim executives, on-call troubleshooters,** and **full-time soloists** . . .

More recently we have been introduced to the 'new independents' and even the 'plurals'.

Of these various labels, 'contractor' stands out as one of the most established and common, yet the diversity of people it applies to is widening. According to a typical dictionary definition, contractors are people who sign a contract to supply labour and/or materials. Traditionally, the term has applied to self-employed individuals who might term themselves 'tradespeople'. They work in sectors such as engineering, landscaping, safety management, construction, aviation, mining, oil and gas. Historically, the term 'contractor' has strong associations with the IT industry.

In his book *The Elephant and the Flea – Looking backwards to the future* (Hutchinson, 2001), Charles Handy focuses his attention on those freelance consultants who possess a unique bank of intellectual property and a talent for turning bright ideas into commercially viable products and services. Working in the arts, science and business, these individuals are generally the brightest and best in their specialist fields, with a truly unique proposition. Describing them as 'fleas', Handy anticipates that these innovators will gradually transform their relationship with the 'elephants' – or large organisations that once employed them. Instead of developing and selling their ideas as full-time permanent employees, says Handy, they will exploit their own creativity on their own terms, working singly or in partnership with other freelance consultants. In return for assuming the risk, they will then sell their products and services back to the elephants for a great deal more than they ever earned as a salary.

John Knell, director and co-founder of the Intelligence Agency ideas consultancy, uses 'self-employed professionals' (SEPs) as a catch-all term for Handy's 'fleas'. It is a term that fits neatly with the subjects of this book. Knell argues that SEPs are championing new workplace practices while pioneering more fulfilling lifestyles, reshaping the modern workplace as they reshape modern lives. While acknowledging that SEPs often face problems such as irregular income, red tape and a sense of isolation, Knell claims that their lifestyle 'offers up a heady cocktail of possibilities – control, balance, success, variety, self-expression, self-fulfilment and individuality'.

Interestingly, Knell claims that not only are the most successful SEPs accomplished in their chosen field, but they have a talent for attracting interest from potential clients by presenting the marketplace with a mix of distinctive identities and capabilities.

Consultants

'Consultant' is a term that retains the historical connotations of authority, experience and skill evoked by its dictionary definition: 'a specialist who gives expert advice or information'.

'Consultant' is a generic term found across all sectors, professions and trades. There are management consultants, medical consultants, IT consultants, business process consultants, organisational change consultants and HR consultants – to name just a few.

A consultant can act as an adviser, an implementer, or both. Consultants are external to the client's organisation and are hired for their particular expertise for a specific period. Historically, the term 'consultant' bestowed a certain status and *gravitas* on an individual, acknowledging the strength of his or her intellect and knowledge. More recently, however, its increasingly widespread use has tended to devalue the term's power. It is often used to disguise any culturally unacceptable associations with selling. For example, make-up counters are no longer staffed by shop assistants but beauty consultants.

Interims

Some would argue that distinguishing between the various types of non-permanent employees is largely a question of semantics. The semantics debate is particularly intense among those who are loosely grouped together under the banner marked 'interim manager' or 'interims'. Many senior members of this community are now keen to distance themselves from the term 'interim manager' altogether, arguing that their brand has been devalued over recent years by an influx of middle managers to their ranks. Others argue that the term has simply been hyped into a brand so that the people who use it can charge more for their services.

The debate is spawning numerous alternative terms – company doctors, transition managers, change managers, continuity managers, turnaround professionals, among other variations. This type of discussion is healthy enough. Apart from anything else, it demonstrates how rich and varied the community is becoming, and how important its members have become to organisations confronting the challenge of constant change. And, of course, the concern over labels is also driven by a desire among senior members of the interim community to differentiate themselves and preserve their day rates.

Qualities that define a successful interim

In their book *Interim Management: The new career choice for senior managers* (Aveton Books, 2nd edition, 2005), Dennis Russell and Ian Daniell describe interims as the 'natural independents', and list their attributes as:

- a strong desire to own their own business
- an identified niche
- a growing, busy target market
- many influential contacts and a demonstrable competence and reputation in that market
- a credible ability to walk into a problem situation and produce a solution calmly and quickly
- financial independence – an ability to survive up to a year without further income
- psychological independence.

These factors suggest that the search for a new catch-all term is unlikely to produce a permanent result. Meanwhile, the terms currently on offer are becoming largely interchangeable. But according to Nick Robeson, chairman of the Interim Management Association, the semantics are largely irrelevant to clients.

> *That's because people who make a success of performing an interim management role invariably share a common DNA that transcends labels.*

For a start, says Nick, they are professional managers. Obvious, perhaps, but sometimes overlooked in the heat of the debate. Secondly, interims are not management consultants. Unlike management consultants, they do not simply leave clients with a set of recommendations – they actually implement them. And unlike management consultants, interims have full operational control over a whole business or a specific part of a business.

> *Comfortable in a crisis, successful interims share a talent for galvanising people into action and unlocking their talent to achieve change. In fact, many clients who use interims rely on them as indispensable to the change process. They can apply their skills to start-ups, mergers and acquisitions, rapid growth programmes, change management and transition; crisis management, turnarounds and closures; absence cover, coaching and mentoring.*

Freelance consultants with a talent for making change happen

As more organisations realise they have to adapt to survive, a growing number are turning to specialist freelance consultants to implement internal change programmes. London-based Boyden Interim Management has identified the key skills that freelance consultants need to ensure change programmes deliver results.

Table 1 | Change management and freelance consultants' skills

Common traps – consistent mistakes and omissions	Assimilation skills – critical management tasks for establishing long-term success	Enablers – personal qualities to be successful
Come in too soon with the answers	Ask questions and listen, listen, listen	Openness to feedback
Stick with the existing team too long	Establish priorities	Cultural sensitivity
Attempt too much too soon	Secure early wins	Flexibility of management style
Are captured by the wrong people	Build personal credibility	Coalition-building
Fall prey to 'successor syndrome'	Gain broad commitment and support	Unlimited time and efficiency
Fail to seek advice or counsel	Build a political base	Emotional resilience
Fail to seek advice or counsel	Lay a foundation for sustained improvement	Effective coping strategies
Fall behind the learning curve	Take steps to change the culture	Personal preparation
Become isolated and invisible	Get orientated quickly	Ability to create a strategic vision

Source: Boyden Interim Management Limited

Today's interims tend to have a minimum of seven years' experience at senior or middle management level, ranging from managing director or director level to head of function. They are in their present role because they have made a career choice – not because they are filling in between other jobs. Their daily rates generally start at £500 per day, and clients are spending £500 million on their services annually. While there is no upper age limit, interims are seldom under 35. There is a tendency among hiring organisations to parachute interims down one rank from the highest rank they reached as a permanent employee.

Whatever their age and rank, all successful interims can demonstrate a proven history of consistently delivering project after project. Some interims are generalists whereas others may specialise in a particular sector or function.

When to use an interim executive

Interim executives work for a wide range of organisations, from small and medium enterprises (SMEs) through to FTSE companies, and cover the following areas:

Operations	General management	Sales
Logistics	Business development	Planning
Finance	Marketing	Advertising
Tax	IT strategy and implementation	Supply chain
Treasury	Human resources	Procurement
Audit	Management assessment and	Purchasing
Risk management	development	Quality assessment
IT operations	Coaching and mentoring	and quality control
Compliance	Communication	Manufacturing

Source: Boyden Interim Management Limited

Many are women. Consummate networkers, they are astute judges of character with an unerring knack for identifying where an organisation's talent lies. There has been a recent rise in the number of younger people choosing to go independent.

The growth in demand for interims from all backgrounds reflects the fact that there are more people in the job market who fit the profile and have a demonstrable track record of achievement.

Highly talented and often restless for the next challenge, successful interims are, in Nick Robeson's opinion, the very last people that any organisation should employ on a permanent basis.

Freelancers

Freelancing: a statistical overview

In their report *Freelancing in marketing and creative services – trends and issues* (published in 2005 in association with the London-based freelance resourcing agency Xchangeteam), researchers at the Leeds Business School explored numerous aspects of the freelance character. An overview of their findings includes the following:

- Freelancing is a long-term career choice – 42 per cent intend to continue freelancing over the next five years. Only 15 per cent want to return to full-time employment.
- Freelancing is conducted at a senior level by the majority of respondents (60 per cent at either manager or director level).
- Freelance consultants work either at an office location (30 per cent) or at a combination of home and office (35 per cent).
- Nearly half the sample have seen their income increase over the past year.
- Eighty per cent of the 662 freelance consultants surveyed are aged 25 to 45. The biggest single grouping of freelance consultants was aged between 31 and 35.
- Freelancing is civilised – the majority of respondents work less than 40 hours per week.
- Studies from other disciplines highlight the importance of networks for freelance consultants. Over half the sample are members of professional associations; 80 per cent are members of informal networks.
- Women are more likely than men to choose freelancing to provide control, reduce stress and avoid office politics. They, more than men, also see it as a means to increase their range of experience. In contrast, men are significantly more likely to have chosen freelancing because they wanted to set up their own business or as a career choice following redundancy.

The original 'freelancers' were medieval knights who sold their fighting skills to the highest bidders on the battlefields of Europe. The term first appeared as two words in books by Middle Age revivalists such as Sir Walter Scott during the nineteenth century. Although the loyalty of freelancers generally lasted no longer than the battle in hand, their good reputation depended squarely on delivering results – and, of course, their performance was easily measured.

Despite their professionalism, the reputation enjoyed by the original freelancers was somewhat compromised down the centuries by the mercenaries and soldiers of fortune who succeeded them. By the mid-nineteenth century, the term 'freelancer' was commonly applied to politicians who moved from cause to cause. In some quarters, the image of disloyalty and unreliability that these individuals created is alive and well to this day.

This is clearly unfair. In the centuries preceding the advent of the welfare state, many of the most respected professionals – including lawyers, doctors and teachers – operated on a freelance basis. Nowadays, there are signs that history has come full circle as a growing number of professionals, notably dentists, are opting out of government-run institutions such as the National Health Service and reclaiming their freelance status as members of independent professional groups.

Acknowledging this trend, Charles Handy divides freelancers into two groups: those who sell their time, and those who sell a product in the form of intellectual property. According to his definition, freelancers who sell time:

- fit into the client organisation's team
- comply with the organisation's rules and regulations

- are hired for their track record and skills
- require tailored management.

Freelancers selling a product are:

- true independent workers who take risk of delivery
- creators of a product that is unique and personal
- reputation-led and indifferent to factors such as age
- idiosyncratic non-conformists who dislike hierarchies
- best left to work alone with minimal management interference.

In other words, freelancers who belong to the second group tend to be solo operators who inject a high degree of individuality into their work. Those in the first group integrate more closely into the client organisation and their work generally follows a more conventional pattern.

The rise of the freelancer as brand

The Internet is a potent driver behind the Me Inc. phenomenon among freelancers. At the top end of the freelance market, sharp and innovative operators are using increasingly affordable and accessible web technology to promote themselves as a brand before a global audience. Given the low investment levels, the returns can be significant – as the independent journalist, commentator, author and public speaker Richard Donkin verifies:

> *When I left full-time employment with the* Financial Times, *I had years of experience and acres of cuttings to prove it. But as a newcomer to freelancing, I needed to learn a new set of business skills such as marketing, negotiating, selling and pricing.*
>
> *I soon discovered that there is no shortage of work out there and finding it is not a problem. But if you want to be taken seriously as a freelance consultant and enjoy the work you do, it is essential that you are selective about the type of work you accept.*

In Donkin's view, those with the greatest choice over the work they accept are those who are best able to establish themselves as a brand. Once the market understands the type of work they excel at, the right sort of commissions will follow. 'I was relatively slow at using the Internet to create my own brand,' he admits. 'But richarddonkin.com has certainly been a very effective shop window. To use a fishing analogy, the site has acted as bait, slowly but surely attracting the right type of fish.'

Donkin – who writes a regular fishing column for the *Financial Times* – agrees that most freelance consultants who are successful at transforming themselves into a brand are invariably people with rare intellectual property to sell and a compelling USP. By creating a brand identity and a reasonable niche, they are able to leverage the value of their intellectual property significantly. 'But it is always important that whatever you do is compatible with the brand you have created.'

Accomplished team players

Whatever their degree of integration, many of the best freelancers – although individualists – know how to thrive in a team-based environment, most conspicuously in sectors such as film, broadcasting and advertising. Here, bespoke multi-disciplined teams are brought together to realise a specific brief before disbanding. Combining the complementary strengths of each member, these creative powerhouses consistently achieve results that make them far more than the sum of their individual parts. The benefits to the hiring organisation are enormous. Not only are quality and flexibility levels high, but costs are relatively low. Rather than spending dead money on overheads, organisations pay for talent specifically selected to meet their objectives.

Freelancers are now taking the team concept one step further by forming networks. Invariably web-based and often global, freelance networks operate according to formal arrangements under which invited members are expected to cross-refer business to the group. Depending on the brief, members will work together on a complete project or divide up separate parts of a project among sub-groups. Like teamworking, the strength of networking lies in its ability to achieve the optimum blend of skills to meet a specific challenge. And like teamworking, networking is highly cost-effective and supremely flexible.

Consultants, interims and freelancers share much in common. The three terms, which are becoming broadly interchangeable, are separated only by tradition and history. Each term has been adopted by different sectors, industries or functions.

In the interests of clarity, this book uses the term **freelance consultant** to cover all three groups. We define 'freelance consultants' as:

- professional people who provide an organisation with a pre-defined talent, service(s) or skill(s)
- people who are not permanent employees
- people who work outside an organisation's established employee pay scales for an agreed fee, commonly based on a day rate
- people who work independently of corporate frameworks and outside its hierarchies without the associated status, promotion prospects or job titles
- people who bear risk.

The different types of freelance consultant

In their report *Freelancing in marketing and creative services – trends and issues* (published in 2005 in association with freelance resourcing agency Xchangeteam), researchers at the Leeds Business School explored the freelance identity in more depth, and considered whether or not definite 'types' of freelance consultant could be identified. The research covered three basic areas: work–life balance, the freelance life, and personal attributes. Data analysis revealed three basic types of freelance consultant:

Work-driven freelance consultants

These freelance consultants are heavily focused on their working life. They are very comfortable with their professional role; they find it rewarding and feel it enhances their personal development. They feel respected and valued by their clients and their profession; the work they undertake allows them to both build a career path and keep up to date with their own skills development. They are satisfied with both their work practices and their salary.

Self-driven freelance consultants

Self-driven freelance consultants' first point of reference is their own character. They are self-motivated, competitive, confident and ambitious. Perhaps correspondingly, they always focus on making their best effort. They are also the type of person who tries to squeeze a lot into their day, working and living at a fast pace and juggling several things at once.

Unsurprisingly, the work-driven and self-driven types are moderately – but significantly – related to each other. That is, those who score highly on the work-driven scale are more likely to score highly on the self-driven scale.

Stress-bitten freelance consultants

Like work-driven freelance consultants, stress-bitten freelance consultants are also heavily focused on work, but it is primarily a source of stress rather than having a positive effect on their lives. These people find their life difficult to manage. They feel stressed, worry about work, and find it difficult to switch off even when at home. As a result, work tends to dominate their lives and they find it hard to give what they perceive as adequate time to family requirements. These freelance consultants seem to be a quite separate group of people from the other two types, and their feelings reflect some of the negative findings about freelance life discovered in earlier work.

Having defined our terms, it is worth commenting that while researching this book, we found that understanding among hiring organisations of how to get the best from freelance consultants was surprisingly weak. Perhaps this is because, until relatively recently, becoming a freelance consultant was regarded as a negative move. During the late 1980s and early 1990s, for example, the freelance community was dominated by middle managers and executives who were made redundant during the first wave of corporate cutbacks. Now, however, freelancing is valued as an empowering alternative to the constraints of permanent employment and a career option in its own right.

HOW TO RECOGNISE A SUCCESSFUL FREELANCE CONSULTANT

In our experience, successful freelance consultants typically combine a range of complementary and sometimes contrasting qualities. Although they are often consummate team players, they also work well alone under their own initiative. They are often diplomatic and sensitive listeners, acting as useful sounding-boards and valuable sources of objective guidance. At the same time, they invariably choose to remain aloof from office politics.

To put it another way: they know how to play the corporate game without taking their eye off the task in hand.

Freelance consultants often have a gift for building strategic working relationships with key people at short notice This process demands a combination of sharp intuition and strong communication skills – two more strengths that characterise successful freelance consultants – along with an ability to self-market and network.

Their other strengths typically include strong analytical skills and a personality driven by results. After all, they are only as good as their last job. Which also means that they are motivated by achieving goals rather than galvanised by the prospect of winning promotion or a higher status among peers.

This mindset often incorporates a creative streak that can sometimes border on the maverick. Freed from corporate conventions, freelance consultants are frequently the people who ask awkward questions, demand smarter answers – and inspire breakthrough solutions.

They are largely innovative, mentally agile problem-solvers whose principal currency is knowledge. They prefer to work for clients rather than a boss and cherish the freedom that comes with working outside a corporate hierarchy. Above all, they have an overriding confidence in their own abilities.

They are excellent time-managers, who know how to get the best results in whatever time-frame they are given. They also know how to instil this discipline in the people they work with.

In our experience, successful freelance consultants usually demonstrate a combination of the following qualities:

- *motivated* – Freelance consultants know that they are only as good as their last assignment.

- *organised* – Freelance consultants are accomplished at prioritising objectives, managing time and setting limits. They regard pressure as an occupational hazard because they can find themselves pulled in conflicting directions by different clients and different parts of the hiring organisation.

- *assertive* – The most effective freelance consultants are often the most assertive – and assertiveness is essential if they are to stay focused on objectives and timescales.

- *confident* – By definition, being a freelance consultant is less secure than permanent employment. Successful freelance consultants are not distracted by uncertainty. In fact, most thrive on it.

- *questioning* – The best freelance consultants are not afraid to ask questions, especially if the questions are obvious or awkward. Curiosity is necessary to ensure the consultants really understand the brief.

- *credible* – Good freelance consultants have a track-record of delivering results.
- *flexible* – The ability to adapt to new cultures, people and assignments is an essential freelancing skill. Freelance consultants who can't adapt don't survive very long.
- *self-disciplined* – Achieving results without being micro-managed is fundamental to being a successful freelance consultant.
- *objective* – A freelance consultant's objectivity can add significant value to the way an organisation operates.

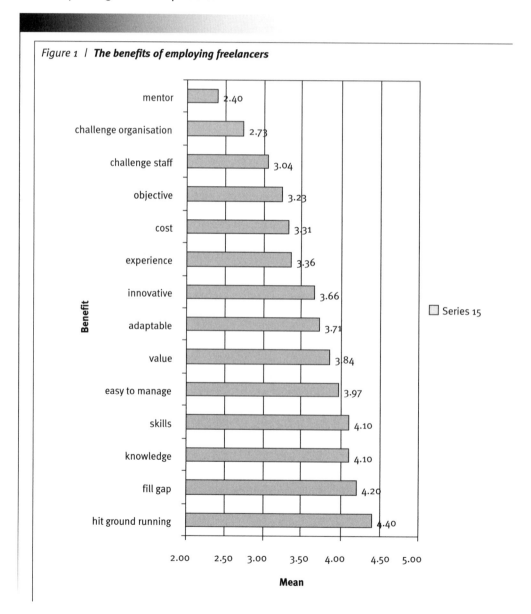

Figure 1 | **The benefits of employing freelancers**

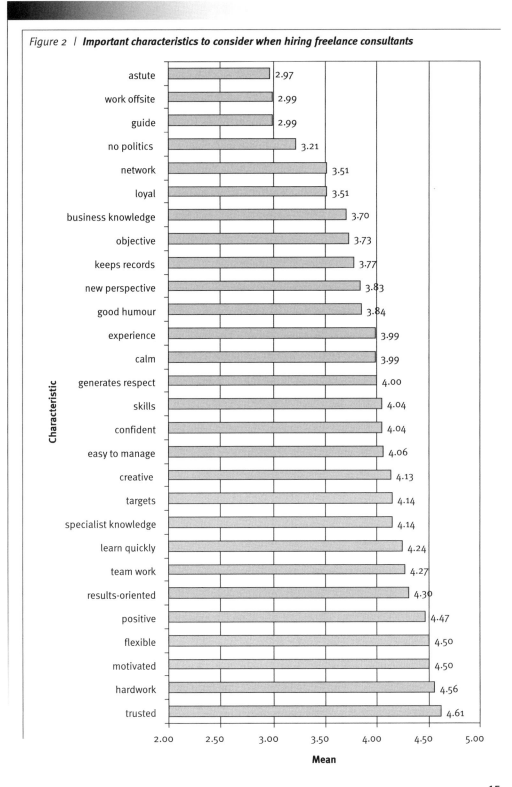

Figure 2 | *Important characteristics to consider when hiring freelance consultants*

What do organisations value in a freelance consultant?

During the course of their research, the Leeds Business School team asked hiring organisations about the benefits of using freelancing consultants (see Figure 1 on page 14). Hirers valued most of all the freelancers' ability to hit the ground running, to fill a current resource gap and their up-to-date knowledge. It was also important that they were easy to manage, had specialist skills, provided value for money and were able to be innovative. The fact that freelancers were a transparent cost to the organisation and could provide an objective view of organisational issues was moderately important.

The ability to get the job done translates into a number of personal characteristics (see Figure 2 on page 16). At the top of the list came trustworthiness, a hardworking nature and motivation. Confidence, a positive attitude, the ability to learn quickly and flexibility were all extremely important.

Other qualities that hirers look for include diverse skills, relevant experience, specialist knowledge, the ability to teamwork, as well as good humour, creativity, calmness and an ability to win respect from permanent staff.

Slightly less critical were a freelance consultant's ability to demonstrate a good all-round understanding of the business and provide a new perspective. From an administrative viewpoint, good record-keeping, the ability to meet targets, and being easy to manage were all sought-after characteristics.

Hirers are much less extreme when it comes to identifying the disadvantages of using freelance consultants. They had moderate problems with the fact that freelance consultants might not be part of the permanent team and therefore demonstrate limited commitment. Nor were hirers unduly concerned if freelance consultants were not familiar with the organisational culture or strategy.

The expense of hiring a freelance consultant is regarded as a problem, although this may or may not be significant in terms of the overall hiring decision, since respondents also recognise the value for money they provide.

The 2005 report found that from the hirer's perspective, there were no clear trends in the current or future use of freelance consultants. Short-term use seemed the only consistent factor. This was also reflected in how they are being appraised or reviewed on performance. Informal reviews are the norm for most respondents (44 respondents, or 63 per cent), although some do use project milestones and specific targets (45 respondents, or 64 per cent) and 19 respondents (27 per cent) say they measure performance against contractual obligations. However, it should be noted that while informality dominates, most respondents do use more than one system of appraisal.

Hirers are consistently underestimating their use of freelance consultants. There appears to be a trend that when looking forward, client respondents tend to be slightly more pessimistic about the number of freelance consultants they expect to hire in the next year. This may be explained by the unpredictability of the roles the freelance consultants fill or a lack of forward planning in busy organisations.

Demand for freelance consultants is driven primarily by organisational and work dynamics rather than by internal or external finances. Two-thirds of the sample say that neither internal profitability nor external conditions are a factor in their decision to hire. For the remainder of the sample, more freelance consultants are hired when profitability is higher and economic conditions more positive.

HOW MANY PEOPLE IN THE UK ARE FREELANCE?

There are today 3 million organisations with no employees in Britain. Add together the formally self-employed, people in micro-businesses and temporary workers and you have roughly a third of the labour force.

Charles Handy, author and academic, quoted in the *Financial Times*

Current estimates put the number of employed UK workers at around 28.5 million. Of these, 86 per cent (24.6 million) are employees and 74 per cent (21.17 million) work full-time (Office of National Statistics, 2005 Labour Market Statistics).

But a growing number of people in the UK workforce do not match the typical profile of the permanent full-time employee. In a workforce of 28.5 million, 3.64 million people (13 per cent) are currently self-employed, which is 1 million more than in 1984. However, this is only part of the picture. To assess trends in the UK labour market accurately, it is important to consider the 7 million part-time workers who make up 24 per cent of the workforce, and temporary workers who make up 7 per cent of the workforce.

It is equally important to take into account the 3.1 million people setting up micro-businesses that have no employees, and the 2.2 million people setting up businesses with no more than four employees. Together, they make up 11.2 per cent and 7.9 per cent of the workforce respectively. Because these people incorporate their businesses, they effectively disguise the fact that they are actually self-employed. As the author and academic Charles Handy has pointed out in conversation with Emma Brierley:

Many freelance consultants are invisible in the economy. The fact is that the Government's Labour Force Survey doesn't ask the right questions. You have to be very careful with statistics, because they can conceal what is actually happening.

Why do freelance consultants go freelance?

In October 2005, a research team at the Leeds Business School – part of Leeds Metropolitan University – published a report entitled *Freelancing in marketing and creative services – trends and issues*, in association with the specialist freelance resourcing agency Xchangeteam. Among other issues, the report explored what motivated people to choose the freelance option.

Presented with a range of reasons, respondents were asked to indicate how important each was in their decision to go freelance. The reasons selected as most important for choosing to freelance were to have more choice and more control over work, closely followed by the need to have a better quality of life.

In respect of the quality of the work they were doing, respondents said that increasing the variety and challenge of the work they were doing as well as increasing their range of experience was also important. More general work-related considerations were the possibility of making more money and to improve working conditions and avoid office politics.

Figure 3 | ***Reasons cited as important for opting to go freelance***

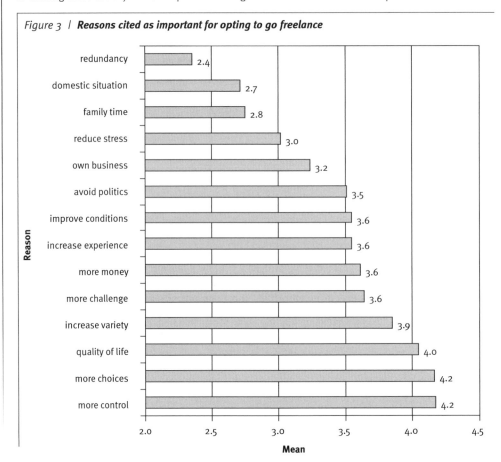

THE ALL-ROUND APPEAL OF GOING FREELANCE

The freelance model is certainly a great leveller and appeals to a broad cross-section of demographic categories, cutting across age, gender and race in an expanding range of sectors and industries. A growing number of women are embracing the freelance model as a way of striking the elusive balance between their professional ambitions and their family commitments. Many choose this way of working because of the freedom and flexibility it gives them to choose what they work on, how they work, when they work, and how long they work.

However, child-rearing is only one trigger for adopting the freelance option. *Harvard Business Review* in March 2005 noted that those women who opted out of jobs in business, banking and finance were motivated more by *dissatisfaction* than by family responsibilities. Women were found to be uncomfortable with organisational politics, the lack of networks and the sense of isolation at senior levels, and are frustrated at the preconceptions inherent in male-dominated companies. A new book, *A Woman's Place is in the Boardroom: The business case* by Jacey Graham and Peninah Thomson (Palgrave Macmillan, 2005), speaks of a 'basic incompatibility between corporate cultures and modern women'.

Increasingly, women are opting to take control of their own destiny rather than continually fighting the 'glass ceiling' syndrome and ending up pigeonholed or sidelined by corporate life. This is hardly surprising given the statistics: in the UK, women hold just 23 per cent of senior positions in the civil service and only 9 per cent of senior positions in business. To make matters worse, they are still paid 19 per cent less than their male counterparts (November 2004 Demos report on disorganisation, *Why Future Organisations Must Loosen Up*; see H. McCarthy, *Girlfriends in High Places*, Demos, 2004, and *Labour Market Trends*, Vol.110, No.12).

Freelancing gives women the opportunity to explore new, interesting avenues outside the confines of status and career path. It gives them greater choice and increased variety in what they do. As one female freelance consultant commented: 'There is no limitation on self-development' (Leeds Business School/Xchangeteam research).

Similarly, freelancing is popular among older professionals because it enables them to 'downsize' their careers. With grown-up families and financial security, they are choosing to leave the 9-to-5, five-days-a-week treadmill. For many seniors, freelancing is driven less by economics and more by maintaining interests and contacts, and having the time to pursue multiple interests. Older freelance consultants tend to be the true 'portfolio workers': seeking to combine personal hobbies such as travel, new interests and philanthropy with their traditional work.

This trend is not lost on organisations that are keen to access highly skilled and experienced individuals who are relatively expensive to employ on a full-time, permanent basis but represent value for money as a freelance consultant.

As the Government looks for ways to encourage older workers to work for longer and legislation outlaws age discrimination, the freelance option is likely to grow in popularity for the older age-group.

Young people, especially graduates, are playing a major role in spreading the freelance mindset. They are entering the job market at a time when the distinction between freelance and permanent working is becoming increasingly blurred. Indeed, recent research by the Work Foundation has revealed that a growing number of young people simply regard permanent employment as a variation on freelancing. They think of themselves as independent workers who will only work for an organisation provided the job suits their life-plan.

In their recent publication, *Working in the Twenty-First Century*, Michael Moynagh and Richard Worsley (Economic Research Council, 2005) suggest that this attitude arises from the fact that young people today are better educated than their parents and grandparents. They are therefore more confident. According to the authors:

> *As prosperity has increased, consumer choice widened and 'deference' gone out of fashion, [young people] have come to expect more autonomy. Often they are more IT 'savvy' than their elders, leaving them better placed to seize self-employment opportunities created by the knowledge economy.*

Moynagh and Worsley conclude that changing attitudes could encourage more self-employment. Indeed, a Prince's Trust survey in 2000 found that two-fifths of 11- to 16-year-olds had decided they were going to work for themselves.

In their publication, *The Independents – Britain's new cultural entrepreneurs*, Charles Leadbeater and Kate Oakley (Demos, 1999) identify three factors that are helping to foster the freelance mindset among young people: technology, values and economics. Having grown up with technology, say the authors, the Independents feel empowered rather than frightened by it. Once upon a time, computers were designed to benefit large organisations. Now they are designed to enrich the lives of individuals, creatively and commercially.

Leadbeater and Oakley point out that the Independents are typically children of the Thatcher years, brought up by parents who lived through the social upheavals of the 1950s and 1960s. As a result, 'They are anti-establishment, anti-traditionalist and in respects highly individualistic: they prize freedom, autonomy and choice.' These are exactly the values that predispose young people towards pursuing self-employment and entrepreneurship in a spirit of self-exploration and self-fulfilment.

As for economics, Leadbeater and Oakley explain that the Independents came to the job market at a time when large organisations were downsizing and jobs-for-life were becoming a thing of the past. For them, 'Self-employment and entrepreneurship became a more realistic option.'

If organisations are to capitalise on the manifest benefits of hiring freelance consultants, they would be well advised to take note of young people's changing attitudes to work and embed a freelance-friendly culture throughout their structures.

Some experts even argue that organisations must learn to manage all their employees just as they manage freelance consultants. We address this argument more fully in the final chapter of this book when we consider the future of freelancing.

The freelance mindset is certainly thriving across an expanding diversity of sectors and industries. Freelance journalists (see the Case study below), a fixed feature in the newspaper business, now ply their trade in other media such as radio and TV. Here, they work alongside actors, singers, musicians, dancers and other professional entertainers who rely on the expertise of backstage professionals who are equally used to working on a project-by-project basis.

CASE STUDY

Fleet Street: defining the freelance mindset

The media in general and newspapers in particular are among the toughest places to prove your freelance credentials. Freelance journalists have been a fixed feature in newspaper offices for decades. According to News International's Andy Jones, they are likely to remain so.

'By their nature, newspapers are driven by the latest news – which means every day is going to be different,' says Andy, who was responsible for managing freelance rosters for *The Sun*. 'Since unpredictability is an occupational hazard, it is essential that we are able to "road test" people before taking them on permanently. You can't interview for many journalism roles, especially on a tabloid. So often, success is down to instinct and attitude. Long experience has proved that taking people on as freelancers is the best way to see if they can cut the mustard as permanent staffers.'

Traditionally, UK journalists on provincial titles and trade press publications have freelanced their way into permanent roles on the nationals. It's a tough job in a macho and distinctly non-PC environment where only the toughest survive. Says Andy: 'Management support and planning are minimal. Rotas are only drawn up two or three weeks in advance, which makes life very insecure for freelancers. To get by, many of them have fingers in several pies at once, most commonly by regularly working for more than one newspaper. They're only as good as their last story and reputation is everything.

'When they arrive here, we show them how to use the computer system and that's about it. They are usually given two or three shifts to prove themselves in terms of written ability and attitude. They are very much left to work things out themselves and the pressure is on them to win our trust through the quality of their work. If they don't impress, they're not invited back. If someone shows promise, they may be in line for a permanent job.'

At present, there is concern in the industry that legislation is making freelance journalists too expensive by entitling them to certain benefits. 'We may have to cut back for a while,' predicts Andy, 'but the added pressure this will place on our permanent staff will soon bring back the freelancers. In fact, I doubt newspapers would survive without freelance journalists – the newsroom environment is too unpredictable.'

Nowhere boasts a more concentrated cluster of freelance workers than Hollywood. This creative Mecca draws in talented individuals to work both in front of and behind the camera. Some are employed by the studios, but the vast majority work for themselves. Constantly searching for the next big idea, Hollywood exists on the raw creative energy of talented individuals who come together determined to crack the big time.

Other individuals once regarded as their employer's permanent assets are becoming increasingly freelance in their attitudes. Over recent years, sport has offered many high-profile examples. Once upon a time, a professional footballer would pledge his loyalty to a club for life. In return, his club would reciprocate his loyalty with security while keeping wages relatively low. This endearingly paternal dynamic has virtually disappeared from football altogether, as players routinely transfer their loyalty to the club that pays them the highest wages.

This may infuriate club chairmen and supporters. But their agents would argue that footballers are simply motivated by the same factors that drive people to go freelance in any other sector: supply and demand, the disappearance of jobs for life, and the rise of a fast-moving, team-based, results-driven working culture.

Key point summary

- The terms used to define non-permanent workers are multiplying as rapidly as the flexible working practices they are pioneering.

- Some terms have been part of the language for centuries, others have only been around for a matter of months.

- Their proliferation is a sign of the quiet revolution currently transforming the UK labour market, a revolution that is not necessarily reflected in official statistics.

- The popularity of new working practices is notable among older professionals, women and young people.

- As its title suggests, this book focuses on three groups of non-permanent workers: consultants, interims and freelancers.

- For the sake of clarity, we refer to all three groups as 'freelance consultants'.

- Among other strengths, successful freelance consultants are motivated, organised, assertive, confident, questioning, credible, self-disciplined and objective.

2

The business case for using freelance consultants

WHY FREELANCE CONSULTANTS ARE HERE TO STAY

Of course, there are lies, damn lies and statistics. But the statistics we quote in the last chapter indicate one indisputable truth: freelance consultants are a fixed feature of the UK labour market. What's more, a number of structural, social and economic trends have combined to ensure that they are set to become increasingly important to the economy. As these irreversible trends continue to shape our working lives, the freelance option is likely to play an increasingly influential role in the way organisations manage their human resources – both permanent and non-permanent. We open this chapter by considering some of the drivers behind this shift.

Structural drivers

The rise of freelance working and the proliferation of increasingly powerful information technology are two sides of the same coin.

As the cost and size of emerging technology falls, its power and accessibility rises. This means that more people can now work even more productively from virtually anywhere they choose, provided they have Internet access and a mobile telephone.

In their joint publication *Mobile Working* (2005), the Institute of Directors and Vodafone UK examine the structural impact of mobile technology, arguing that mobile working is already becoming the rule rather than the exception. In 2003, UK professionals spent 25 per cent of their time outside the office, a figure that is set to hit 42 per cent by 2007. Already, laptop sales are exceeding desktop computer sales as organisations recognise how indispensable mobile communications are to saving on the US $8 billion that they lost in dead working time during 2004.

'The message is clear,' state the authors. 'The trend towards flexible working practices is strong and irreversible – and for very good business and lifestyle reasons. The key is for businesses to understand this trend, and to protect their future competitiveness by blending the innovative and evolving technologies with new ways of working.'

Mobile working is yet another factor that is shifting the employer–worker relationship firmly in favour of workers in general and freelance workers in particular. It makes sense for organisations to capitalise on this shift by embracing freelance consultants and accepting the new working conventions that they are pioneering with the help of increasingly sophisticated technology. If they fail to do so, organisations risk closing their doors on many of the most talented, focused and innovative individuals in the workforce.

Social drivers

Many of these individuals are women. Traditionally, they have been responsible for the care and welfare of the family unit. Growing numbers are now combining their traditional role with full- or part-time jobs. In their recent publication *Working in the Twenty-First Century*, Michael Moynagh and Richard Worsley (Economic Research Council, 2005) note that only 40 per cent of women have 'standard jobs', which they define as jobs in which individuals work at the employer's premises during the day and for 30 to 48 hours a week.

The drivers behind this trend are complex and varied, although economic pressures invariably play their part. Beyond the detailed arguments lies the fact that women will continue to pioneer new ways to combine work and family while avoiding the 'glass ceiling' syndrome.

Because women now play such an important role in the workplace, organisations must respond to their demands with more flexible, family-friendly working practices – including the freelance model.

As people become more mobile and their talents become more marketable, their loyalty towards employers is diminishing. Several factors account for this. For a start, employers are not able to guarantee employees the same levels of long-term job security that many people took for granted during the post-war years. Nowadays, the chances of landing a job for life are disappearing from the workplace as quickly as Tipp-Ex and typewriter ribbons.

Rather than resisting these changes, forward-looking organisations are capitalising on this by becoming adaptive organisations, embracing a mix of working models – from the traditional 9-to-5 model to flexible and freelancing models. This trend is confirmed by some convincing statistics. For example, in their study of 2,000 UK establishments, *Managing to Change? British Workplaces and the Future of Work*, Michael White, Stephen Hill, Colin Mills and Deborah Smeaton (Palgrave Macmillan, 2004) report that four out of five workplaces used at least one of the following: temporary staff supplied by agencies, their own temporary employees, workers employed on a casual basis, freelance (self-employed) workers, and homeworkers or outworkers.

At the same time, more organisations recognise how much they can benefit from the experience and expertise of older workers, who are particularly suited to the freelance lifestyle. A growing number of men and women over the age of 45 are choosing to extend their careers through more flexible, less conventional working practices. Not only are they keen to contribute their skills and know-how, they know they can do so on their own terms.

Economic drivers

Globalisation and the increased competition it produces is arguably the single most powerful influence on today's economies. Among other impacts, it is having a profound effect on the relationship between businesses and the customers they serve.

As Richard Scase, Professor of Organisational Behaviour at the University of Kent at Canterbury, points out, businesses no longer control the pace of change in their sectors. That power is slowly but surely shifting in favour of the consumer.

To survive this change, businesses have been forced to operate more flexibly and deliver more quickly while satisfying increasingly demanding and discerning customers. At the same time, customers and markets are becoming more volatile and unpredictable. To

The hiring curve

Hiring freelance consultants minimises risk during periods of economic uncertainty and low consumer confidence by enabling organisations to cut overheads if business falls. As Figure 4 below illustrates, demand for freelance consultants tends to follow a U-bend model, shadowing the economic cycles of boom and bust, recession and recovery.

Figure 4 / **The U-bend model of demand for freelance consultants**

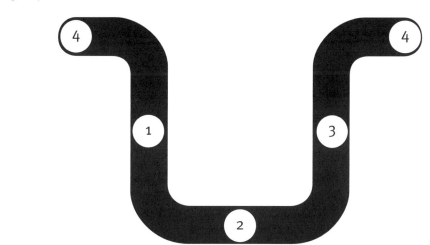

1 Freelancers are often the first to go when companies hit hard times.
2 Companies begin reducing staff headcount through redundancy programmes and demand for freelance consultants is minimal as they reduce activity levels.
3 As business confidence grows and budgets are reinstated, demand for freelancers can grow very rapidly as companies still remain wary of increasing their fixed costs.
4 Once economic equilibrium returns, demand becomes steadier as freelance consultants are brought in for a wide range of reasons such as project management, work overload, specialist skills, etc.

keep meeting people's needs, organisations are under relentless pressure to innovate. Between 1992 and 2000, 30 per cent of the top 50 UK companies were engaged in large-scale reorganisation every year by the end of the decade as against 20 per cent at the beginning.

Figures such as these help to explain why people with ideas are in such high demand. And because many of the most imaginative innovators in the job market work freelance, they are likely to become even more sought after as the forces of globalisation intensify. Demand is likely to grow further because employing a large permanent workforce in a time of permanent change simply does not make economic sense. Instead, hiring freelance consultants is an effective way of mitigating the risks associated with the prevailing turbulence.

Commenting on the drivers behind the freelance boom, Professor Scase says:

> *In a global marketplace, what sells today will not necessarily sell tomorrow. Which means that every business must re-invent itself continuously, working quickly to innovate and produce. In practice, the one strength that distinguishes a business from its competitors is talent. And because the most talented people are so often freelance, businesses have no choice but to use them.*

Meanwhile, the shortage of skills and talent is also intensifying. As demand outstrips supply, employers are offering potential recruits increasingly attractive salaries and packages. Before long, skilled and talented people will also expect to be offered flexible working options alongside other incentives. Already, a growing number of people are choosing to benefit from these options by going freelance. It is quite possible that the freelance community will eventually become the single most accessible and abundant source of real creative talent.

THE CASE FOR USING FREELANCE CONSULTANTS

The freelance model: potential advantages

- Flexes with business peaks and troughs
- Accesses specialised skills fast
- Drives change
- Injects energy and creativity
- Adds a fresh perspective
- Transfers skills
- Maximises cost-efficiencies
- Transparent costs increases budgetary control
- Lowers risks of employer obligations (eg redundancy)
- Provides access to the best talent.

Having established that freelance consultants are here to stay, we can now examine the business case for hiring them. Because no two organisations are identical, we have confined this overview to assessing the generic arguments for taking the freelance option.

Not all arguments will apply to all organisations. There is, however, a widespread need across all sectors for clarity on the financial impact of using freelance consultants. This is an area where we have placed particular emphasis – and drawn some unexpected conclusions.

Freelance consultants maximise your flexibility and control

Correctly managed, freelance consultants can deliver the levels of speed, skill and flexibility that are essential to an organisation's capacity to function in a faster, more fragmented and less predictable environment.

Hiring freelance consultants gives organisations tighter control over their fixed permanent payroll costs while minimising the exposure to growing legal and regulatory risks related to permanent employees.

In addition, hiring freelance consultants is a proven way of dealing with high workloads during busy times but minimising overheads once the pressure eases. Not only does this flexibility enable freelance-aware organisations to meet current demand, it also allows them to move beyond day-to-day fire-fighting to anticipate future requirements in a more proactive manner.

The flexing principle is tried and tested in sectors where business has traditionally been seasonal – for example, construction and agriculture. However, it now applies to a growing number of organisations in a growing number of sectors. As we have established, globalisation is just one of many factors driving this trend. In addition, market trends are becoming more unpredictable as market sectors fragment. So not only is it becoming more difficult to anticipate staff numbers, anticipating what skills they will need is no longer always straightforward either. And all the time, market forces are rapidly compressing the space between peaks and troughs.

As Professor Scase points out:

> *Freelance consultants now work at the very highest levels of business. Using freelance consultants means you can match the individual's profile to the leadership style you are looking for. If you're looking to consolidate, bring in someone with a track record for consolidating. If you're looking to grow, hire someone with a track record for growth – and so on. The beauty of the freelance model is that you are not committed to retaining a freelance consultant if they no longer fit the strategy.*

Given the volatile outlook and the need to flex at speed, the arguments in favour of the freelance option begin to sound more compelling. Legally and financially, permanent employees might even begin to look more like risks than assets.

Freelance consultants deliver value for money

When it comes to hiring freelance consultants, achieving value for money involves a trade-off between how much they cost and the level of skill, expertise and knowledge you require – and how quickly. Freelance consultants are by no means a cheap option. Then again, recruiting someone on a permanent basis is not cheap either.

Once you factor in hidden costs that we discuss in detail below, freelance consultants begin to look very good value. Of course, permanent employees can also deliver good value for money. But freelance consultants are generally highly skilled, experienced and motivated, which drives their value high beyond their costs.

Perversely, however, recent research undertaken by MBA students of the London Business School (report by Margarita Koshman and Kendra Thayer, published 2003 by Xchangeteam) indicates that a significant percentage of employers (64.3 per cent) still regard freelance consultants as 'more expensive' or 'much more expensive' than permanent staff. Let us examine the facts – beginning with the issue of hidden costs.

As well as tightening control over headcount, hiring freelance consultants enables organisations to eliminate the hidden costs of employing people on a permanent basis. True enough, freelance consultants typically earn more than permanent staff if their day rates are converted to an annual salary, but their clients will not end up paying employers' National Insurance, statutory sick pay, statutory holiday pay, statutory maternity pay, training costs, equipment costs, administrative support – or any of the other direct and indirect costs associated with permanent employees.

Nor do clients pay freelance consultants the additional benefits that many permanent staff now consider standard. Such benefits might include pensions, private health care and travel costs. In sectors where the demand for skills outstrips supply, permanent staff might expect their remuneration package to include a range of additional perks such as gym membership and childcare allowances. Freelance consultants, on the other hand, are not entitled to any of these benefits.

These costs can be far higher than many employers assume. Indeed, research conducted in the USA estimates that hidden costs can add as much as 40 per cent to a permanent employee's basic salary. In the UK, employers' National Insurance alone adds 12.8 per cent to an employee's basic gross salary while statutory holiday pay adds a further 8.33 per cent.

Clearly, the perception that freelance consultants are an expensive option does not always stand up to scrutiny. In a growing number of instances, they can actually prove more cost-effective than permanent employees. Because they are often among the best in their professional field, freelance consultants often have the skills and experience to scale steep learning curves rapidly with little or no training – eliminating another potentially high hidden cost.

Of course, organisations may well pay an agency fee for a freelancer's services, but this also applies when recruiting permanent staff. But agency fees for a freelance consultant only become due when you are actually using them. Paying them could well be more cost-effective than managing your own freelance roster in-house.

Yet the ability of freelance consultants to win future assignments typically depends on how well they performed on their last assignment. As a result, they bring an energy and focus to their work that can often make them seem more productive than many of the permanent employees they work alongside. This places their hirer in the win-win position of achieving more for less.

An organisation typically pays freelance consultants for an agreed period or until they deliver agreed outcomes, tangible or intangible. Organisations do not pay freelance consultants for downtime as a result of sickness, or under-utilisation that arises because of over-capacity or bad planning. When you factor these elements in, permanent employees can work far less than the average 242 working days per year.

But the value that freelance consultants can add is hardly insignificant. Because they are focused on delivering results, freelance consultants are generally highly motivated. This makes them very efficient and productive. They know how to get things done and are trained to hit the ground running. Better still, their work ethic is often contagious, encouraging employees around them to raise their game and improve organisational performance.

Correctly drawn up, an agreement with a freelance consultant becomes a case study in transparency and accountability. All these factors tend to mean that freelance consultants can deliver greater value for money than permanent staff.

Freelance consultants inject vital creative energy

Geoff Nicol is managing director of Navyblue, a thriving strategic communications group with offices in London and Edinburgh. 'Nothing gives the studio a bigger lift than having a top freelance consultant around the place,' he says. 'At best, the vitality and creativity they bring gives everyone a tremendous buzz.'

These views are widely shared – and understandably so. Typically talented individuals in their chosen fields, freelance consultants often succeed on their ability to originate and execute new ideas. Precisely because they are not part of the corporate fabric, they think without blinkers and bring to bear wide experience gained from working across multiple organisations. Since ideas are the currency of the future, freelance talent is likely to be in demand for a long time to come.

This is not always straightforward. Freelance consultants have chosen to work as independents precisely because they regard corporate norms as a straitjacket. Put simply, freelance consultants can be mavericks with a tendency to ask awkward questions. The author and academic Charles Handy refers to them (in *The Elephant and the Flea*, Hutchinson, 2001) as 'fleas', constantly irritating large organisations, which Handy describes as elephants, into changing their ways. Rather than trying to neutralise it, it is up to organisations to find ways of channelling the fleas' creative energy productively.

Freelance consultants drive organisational change

The Professional Contractors Group (PCG) is the representative body for the UK's freelance small business community. In recent years it has identified a rising demand for freelance consultants specifically among organisations undergoing change. According to Diana Watson, marketing consultant to the PCG:

> *The last thing organisations need during times of change and uncertainty are the obligations and commitments associated with permanent employees.*
>
> *Once the dust has settled on a particular change programme, organisations might choose to consolidate their core headcount by recruiting permanent employees afresh. But in the thick of change, they require individuals capable of negotiating turbulence and delivering results – with minimum delay.*
>
> *These qualities are characteristic of freelance consultants. And because change has become a constant for so many organisations, the need for freelance consultants is likely to become another constant in the workplace.*

By delivering tangible results under challenging conditions, freelance consultants often have a more subtle impact on an organisation's culture. Leading by example during the course of their work, they can often influence permanent staff towards adopting their results-focused mindset. They do not always express this mindset in a very demonstrative fashion, but it often shows in the way they conduct meetings, meet deadlines, organise their time and interact with those around them.

As well as shaping cultures, freelance consultants can influence the management style of the organisations they work for. Organisations that use freelance consultants on a regular basis often discover that they no longer need rigid management structures. Instead, they feel more comfortable with the flat structure that is essential to speeding decisions and maximising agility.

In this respect, freelance consultants are helping to change the traditional relationship that exists between employers and their permanent employees. Until relatively recently, this relationship was loaded in favour of employers, especially those relying on a command-and-control management style. However, the balance of power is now shifting the other way as more permanent employees are given the freedom to unlock their energy and creativity by working more like freelance consultants.

Freelance consultants deliver specialist skills fast

Hiring freelance consultants is arguably the most effective way of accessing specialist skills at short notice for a finite period. Not only does it allow you to hire the best in the business, it also allows you to hire them at the best time for your business.

What's more, you are not obliged to cover the cost of retaining specialist skills in-house when they are not required. By bringing in specialists on a freelance basis, you are creating a project-based culture that encourages results. But there is one important question to consider when using freelance consultants to enhance your skill base: how do you capture their skills and transfer them to your in-house teams?

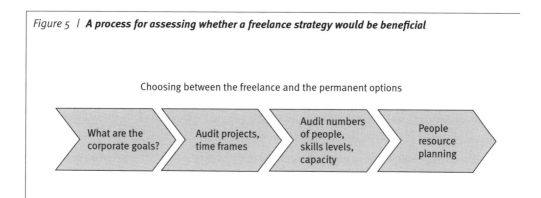

Figure 5 | *A process for assessing whether a freelance strategy would be beneficial*

Choosing between the freelance and the permanent options

What are the corporate goals? → Audit projects, time frames → Audit numbers of people, skills levels, capacity → People resource planning

HOW TO DECIDE WHETHER TO HIRE FREELANCE CONSULTANTS

So far in this chapter we have established that freelance consultants are now a fixed feature of the UK job market, and hiring them offers a number of strong advantages – in the face of major social, structural and economic challenges. To recap: the business case identifies five major benefits of a freelance strategy – maximising flexibility and control, delivering value for money, injecting creativity, driving organisational change, and delivering specialist skills.

Now you need to put a process into your organisation to assess whether or not a freelance strategy would be beneficial or not. Once this is in place you will have all you need to sell the strategy internally. Figure 5 outlines a suggested process that you could follow.

Do freelance consultants support your long-term corporate goals?

If freelance consultants do not support your long-term corporate goals, hiring them may be more trouble than it is worth.

If, on the other hand, they do align with your aims, then thorough planning is still required to strike the optimum balance between your permanent headcount and freelance support.

To decide whether you want to pursue a freelance strategy or not, we suggest that you ask yourself some strategic questions – which should be weighted – along the following lines:

- Is your business subject to peaks and troughs in demand?
- Do you have a large number of defined projects that need to be completed speedily within set timeframes?
- Is your organisation undergoing a transformation, and do you require specialists to drive changes through the organisation?
- Is it difficult to find sufficient talent and/or knowledge in key areas of your organisation?

- Would a pool of freelance talent give you access to better or more suitable skills, experience or contacts?
- Do you need an injection of fresh thinking and creativity to increase productivity?

Evaluate your business needs and resources

Once you have decided your strategic direction, you will then need to decide what you need operationally by following the four steps shown below.

Step 1: Analyse the number of projects and/or the volume of work to be completed over the coming year.

Step 2: Audit your permanent staff to establish numbers, skills and seniority levels. You can audit by project team, division and/or organisation.

Step 3: Create your people resource plan (see Figures 6a–d below) to map your existing people and skills to the anticipated work/projects, thereby identifying the resource gap within a certain timeframe.

Step 4: Having identified the 'resource gap', now you need to make the decision on the balance between increasing your permanent headcount and using 'in-time resourcing' – in other words, hiring freelance consultants.

There could be internal pressure to use any spare capacity on your permanent payroll before considering the freelance option. Take care when dealing with this issue. Problems can arise if you are using permanent staff to complete tasks for which they not suitable just because they are on the payroll. This can become critical if the project in question is complex, specialist or time-sensitive. Your organisation must also weigh the costs of removing people from tasks for which they are suitably qualified and motivated.

---

*Figure 6a | **People resource planning – create a resource plan***

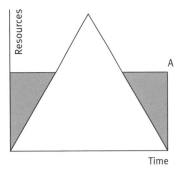

6a: Draw up a resource plan (represented by the triangle) using the information gathered from your audit, listing the skills you require to complete all forthcoming work on schedule. Line A represents the level of your current permanent staffing. Please note that in any level of permanent staffing, there will always be a level of wasted resource as represented by the grey-shaded areas.

*Figure 6b | **People resource planning – identify the resource gap***

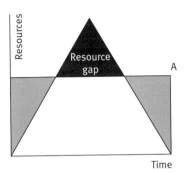

6b: Your resource plan allows you to measure your 'resource gap', which is represented in black. This gap is the difference between the volume of work you need to complete and the number of permanent staff and skills currently available to complete it.

*Figure 6c | **People resource planning – decide whether to employ more permanent people***

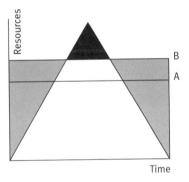

6c: You have two choices. Firstly, you can increase your permanent staffing represented by the level of Line B. However, this does mean that the level at which you under-utilise people may well increase if they are not employed at full capacity. This is a significant hidden cost (see cost model, Table 2 below). What's more, you are still likely to have a resource gap.

Based on the just-in-time (JIT) manufacturing model from the 1970s and 1980s, in-time resourcing involves managing your human resources just as you would manage any other link in your supply chain – applying the same management techniques that are routinely applied to transport or warehousing, for example. In all cases, flexibility, timing and quality are of the essence.

Figure 6d | ***People resource planning – or to opt for 'in-time resourcing'***

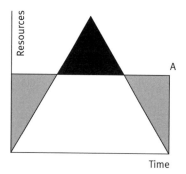

6d: Your second choice involves hiring freelance consultants using an 'in-time resourcing strategy'. This means only hiring freelance consultants when you need them and for as long as you need them, as indicated by the black area.

In summary, in-time resourcing has the potential to deliver the following benefits:

- enhanced flexibility
- closer alignment of skills to requirements
- reduced cost per project
- reduced cost per consultant
- improved project profitability
- increased capacity to take on more work
- improved focus on value-adding activities among key staff
- improved ability to attract the skills and the talent.

Handpicking a select team of talented people to deliver a specific project just in time is a highly effective way of harnessing their commitment, energy and flair. Setting fixed timescales and a clear division of responsibility along agreed reporting lines helps to focus team members' initiative and energy even more sharply. Significantly, it is also an effective way of capturing the loyalty required to mould collective strengths into a powerful creative force that is greater than the sum of its parts.

Indeed, the notion that loyalty is exclusive to permanent employees is well past its sell-by date. There is even a convincing counter-argument to be made: that permanent employees are potentially more vulnerable to complacency, stagnation and 'quick fixes'. By contrast, freelance consultants thrive in a project-based culture, where the emphasis is on achieving targets by a specific date. They are not distracted by office politics and, as a rule, they are not afraid to voice their opinions if priorities begin to change and schedules begin to slip.

Of course, a critical mass of properly managed, motivated and rewarded permanent staff will always be essential to many organisations. But although your permanent staff may be experienced at handling the routine and the familiar, specialist skills are essential to handling the one-off projects that are required to sustain an organisation's competitive edge.

Although it may not make sense to retain these specialist skills on a permanent basis, deploying judiciously selected freelance consultants alongside permanent staff is an effective way of achieving the versatility and flexibility to meet new demands with innovative solutions. And in today's climate, versatility, flexibility and innovation are vital success drivers.

Prepare a cost model as part of your evaluation process

On the cost side of the equation, you need to compare the cost of recruiting a permanent employee against the cost of hiring a freelance consultant. As we have already established, comparing a permanent employee's annual salary with a freelance consultant's annualised day rate does not take into account the hidden costs associated with permanent employees. You therefore need to ensure that you are comparing like with like. The table below itemises the direct and indirect costs associated with both models, allowing a more accurate cost comparison between them. The standard metric to allow you to compare costs is 'average cost per day'. As we suggested earlier in this chapter, you may find the results of this comparison surprising.

*Figure 7 | **What a cost model is for***

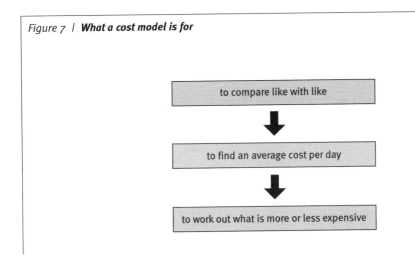

Table 2 | *A cost model, to compare permanent and freelance staff data*

PERMANENT EMPLOYEE DATA	
Total salary costs	
Direct costs (percentage of salary or aggregate £) Taxes (NIC, statutory costs) Additional insurance (medical, dental, life) Pension Direct training Perks (cars, gym membership, subsidised lunches) Agency fees	
TOTAL **direct costs** (percentage of salary or aggregate £)	
Indirect costs Package Total support staff costs (eg IT, admin, finance) Paid rest period p.a.(sickness, holiday, downtime)	
TOTAL **indirect costs** (percentage of salary or aggregate £)	
TOTAL COSTS	
Total increase in costs as a percentage of salary costs	
Total average cost per employee	
Actual working days per year	
Actual employee costs per day	
FREELANCE DATA	
Average daily fee	
Direct costs Taxes paid, if applicable Agency fees	
TOTAL COSTS	
Total increase in costs as a percentage of daily fee costs	
Actual freelancer costs per day	
MORE OR LESS EXPENSIVE?	

To complete the comparison exercise, establish the average daily cost of each employee by dividing his or her total cost by the number of working days in a year. Now you are in a stronger position to decide whether hiring a freelance consultant is more or less expensive than recruiting a permanent member of staff.

There are two other factors to consider when weighing up the comparative costs of hiring a freelance consultant with the cost of employing a permanent employee:

- *Overcapacity*
  To compensate for unpredictable spikes in demand for their products and services, many employers take on too many staff. The cost of employing non-productive staff during idle periods comes directly out of any profits.

- *Replacement costs*
  In many sectors, permanent employees move jobs once every two or three years. The cost of replacing them can add between 4 and 6 per cent to their basic salaries.

Together, overcapacity and replacement costs can add an additional 25 per cent to a permanent employee's basic salary. Overall, indirect costs can mean that a permanent member of staff can cost an employer one and a half times more than his or her pay cheque. As the London School of Business's MBA student researchers concluded: 'In many cases, the total cost difference between permanent and freelance staff is insignificant.'

But establishing costs is only half of the freelance-versus-permanent debate, which must also take into account *value*.

It is worth repeating that hiring freelance consultants is not simply a question of cost. Rather, it is about achieving value for money by having access to the skills, knowledge and talent you need to achieve your business goals.

To sum up, you have evaluated your business requirements, created a people resource plan and established whether to use freelance consultants and/or permanent staff after having produced a cost-benefit analysis.

Armed with your business case, you are now in a stronger position to move towards implementing your in-time resourcing strategy.

HOW TO IMPLEMENT YOUR IN-TIME RESOURCING STRATEGY

*Figure 8 | **Implementing a freelance resourcing strategy***

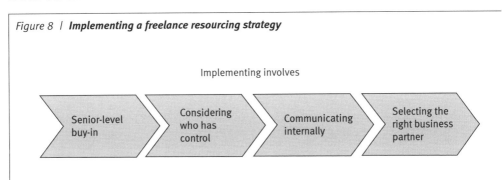

The next challenge is to sell your case to senior decision-makers in your organisation – and win their buy-in.

This, however, is just the start of creating a successful freelance strategy. Having secured the go-ahead, your immediate priorities will include deciding where the ultimate control of your organisation's freelance strategy will lie – with HR, senior management, line management or your procurement function.

In practice, responsibility generally lies with either HR or senior/line management. Typically, procurement's role is to work with whoever actually implements the freelance strategy, helping to establish the optimum supply base. According to Carolyn Murphy, Recruitment and Training Senior Buyer in the procurement team at Tesco:

> *Procurement departments offer buying expertise and supplier management and also enable business units to get a broad understanding of the market they are buying in. Our job is to work in an integrated way with HR.*

Perceptions that procurement teams are only interested in price are not always borne out, although such teams often have a cost-cutting remit. However, it is vital that procurement teams are familiar with the cost-versus-value argument that we outline on pages 35–7.

Table 3 **|** *Establishing who should be in control of a resourcing strategy*

HR	*Procurement*	*Line management*	*Senior management*
PROS			
Understands the people resourcing strategy across the company	*Can set up larger deals so gaining economies of scale*	*Know what they want and what the project entails*	*Know the bigger strategic picture and so understand best what the business needs*
Understands how to hire people – interviewing and the financial and legal frameworks	*Can achieve better value for money which isn't always down to cost*	*Can make decisions quickly*	*Can make decisions quickly*
CONS			
Doesn't always understand what line management needs	*Can focus on cost to the exclusion of quality*	*Don't always understand the bigger picture*	*Can become involved in too much detail*
Can slow down decision-making so weakening business relationships	*Can slow down decision-making so weakening business relationships*	*Don't understand how to hire people/don't have time to do it properly*	*Can be difficult to access*

When buying at the top end of the professional freelance market, talent is scarce, hard to find – and should not be subject to the rules of commodity-buying.

Another priority, often ignored, is communicating your strategy throughout your organisation. For although your senior decision-makers have an important part to play in fostering a freelance-friendly culture, it is the people on the front line of your organisation who make or break it.

Finally, ensure that you select a people resourcing agency capable of working in partnership with you to implement your strategy effectively (see Chapter 5).

Looking ahead, setting regular review points will ensure that the strategy delivers long-term.

WHICH FREELANCE OPTIONS ARE MOST SUITABLE FOR YOUR ORGANISATION?

Assuming that using freelance consultants aligns with your corporate goals, you have a number of freelance options to choose from, and, in practice, they may overlap. To make your choice, you must be clear on the level of commitment that your organisation is prepared to invest.

- *Body-shopping*
  This effectively involves buying individuals. This strategy is most suitable when you only require a limited number of freelance consultants on a one-off ad hoc basis. Although fees tend to be higher, you have complete flexibility because you are not tied into contracts.

- *Bespoke teams*
  This strategy involves forming multi-disciplinary teams of freelance consultants who work together for the duration of a project. It is a cost-effective alternative to the standard service agency model because you are buying the talent without the overhead of the office and administrative functions.

---

*Figure 9 | **Types of freelance strategy and level of commitment***

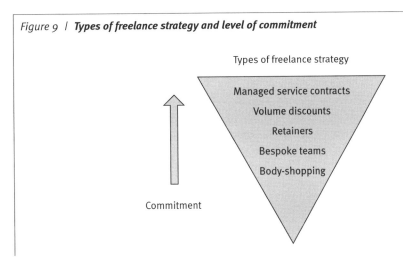

- *Retainers*
  These are paid to highly-prized freelance consultants to secure their services for a specific period of time and/or to prevent them from working for competitors.

- *Volume discounts*
  This strategy is appropriate when you have volume in terms of multiple needs for freelance support. Committing to an agreed volume of business over an agreed period makes it easier to secure fee discounts from agencies and freelance consultants.

- *Managed service contracts*
  In return for cost-savings in your recruitment budget, you appoint a people resourcing agency to take over the management of all your recruitment needs and, if necessary, your HR function. Your appointed agency supplies you with people and also sub-contracts this function to specialist agencies according to your requirements.

Key point summary

- Irreversible structural, social and economic trends mean that freelance consulting is here to stay.

- Adapt to this shift by acknowledging the positives that freelance consultants can bring to your organisation.

- The business case for freelance consultants is founded on flexibility and control, value for money, creativity, organisational change and specialist skills.

- In addition, research indicates that freelance consultants are not necessarily more expensive than permanent employees – but typically deliver outstanding value for money.

- To ensure cost-efficiency and reliable access to talent, plan your people resources as thoroughly as you plan other links in your supply chain.

- Replace quick-fix short-term use of freelance consultants with a long-term flexible strategy based on in-time resourcing.

- Before implementing your strategy, decide who will control it: senior management, line management, HR or procurement – or a combination of all four.

- Decide on the level of commitment your strategy will involve: body-shopping, bespoke teams, retainers, volume discounts or managed service contracts.

3

Evaluating the risks of using freelance consultants

When it comes to integrating freelance consultants, buy-in from senior management is essential. A visible show of their support on Day 1 is imperative. But integration is not always easy to achieve, because there are some people who feel that the arrival of a freelance consultant is a conspicuous demonstration of their own failure. This may or may not be the case, but it is important to acknowledge any problems that do exist in an organisation rather than hiring freelance consultants and then immediately sidelining them.

Janet Morris, Interim Marketing Director

What are the risks associated with using freelance consultants?

Before hiring freelance consultants, it is worth taking steps to ensure you are not exposed to the risks they might bring with them:

- loss of corporate memory
- dilution of corporate brand, value and culture
- loss of corporate control and accountability
- transfer of knowledge to competitors
- poor understanding of the hiring organisation's business
- overload on management resources
- unsettled permanent staff
- increased costs
- compromised client relationships
- lack of commitment.

As the last two chapters have shown, the freelance model offers distinct advantages to hiring organisations. At the same time, there are inherent risks associated with using freelance consultants. In Chapter 7 we examine the management techniques that are most effective at minimising or eliminating these risks. But we devote this chapter to outlining exactly what these risks might involve.

LOSS OF CORPORATE MEMORY

The departure of a freelance consultant could result in the loss of priceless intellectual property and corporate memory. David Coats, Deputy Director of Research at the Work Foundation, regards this as one of the major drawbacks of using freelance consultants. As he points out:

> *The freelance model involves massive transactional costs and takes no account of the loss it inflicts on corporate memory. Often freelance consultants are brought in to solve a particular problem. If they then walk away with the solution, then the organisation has not progressed. In fact, it has gone backwards.*

Preventing this loss is not simply a question of agreeing a watertight contract that takes particular account of copyright and confidentiality, although this is always a good start. Loss prevention also demands rigorous adherence to a robust set of management procedures designed to manage freelance consultants from entry to exit. Most freelance consultants are aware of this issue. One defining mark of a credible freelance consultant is an ability to hand over seamlessly and imprint knowledge on the organisation he or she is leaving. However, you shouldn't assume that freelance consultants all possess this skill. Instead, establish your own systems to ensure that they deliver as much knowledge while they are with you and leave as much of it behind upon departure.

To minimise the risk of corporate amnesia, you might choose to keep freelance consultants away from commercially sensitive projects or work that is critical to your organisation's strategic goals. But this is not always possible or advisable if you wish to sustain your competitive edge. For example, in fast-moving and complex industries such as pharmaceuticals or IT, organisations tend to accept that working on the cutting edge involves bringing on board a wide range of independent or freelance experts. These people typically choose not to work within the hierarchies of large organisations. What's more, a lot of organisations cannot afford to keep such high-calibre brainpower on their permanent payroll.

The key to creating productive relationships with such people lies in negotiating innovative and rewarding contracts that protect your organisation's rights over the freelance consultant's intellectual property wherever necessary. This way, your corporate memory still grows but in a controlled and risk-averse manner.

In future, an organisation's ability to protect its corporate memory will have a significant impact on its success – regardless of what type of person it hires.

DILUTION OF CORPORATE BRAND, VALUE AND CULTURE

There is a strong argument to the effect that if you hire too many freelance consultants, you compromise the purity of your organisation because they are not 'company people' bound together by a common vision, culture and goals. By their very nature, freelance consultants are transient and therefore dilute your shared identity.

There is plenty of evidence to support this argument. Some freelance consultants make no effort to assimilate into a client's organisation, failing to understand its culture and resisting 'the way things are done round here'. Others try too hard. Some freelancers fail to master their clients' reporting procedures and administrative systems. Some fail to inter-relate with permanent staff, stoking resentment.

Then again, good freelance consultants recognise that they share a responsibility to break down barriers, build bridges with permanent employees and work to create a positive working environment from Day 1 of their assignment. And, of course, there are times when an organisation may hire a freelance consultant because it does not want him or her to assimilate, prizing his or her objectivity and ability to achieve change.

The argument in favour of using freelance consultants is hardest to win when an organisation's intangible assets are subjects of the debate. Many organisations are more willing to entrust the routine, the mechanical and the measurable to freelance consultants. Or, at least, they are prepared to have the debate. But an organisation's intangible assets —reputation, profile, brand values, knowledge capital, corporate culture, etc — are often fiercely protected within an inner sanctum accessible exclusively to top management.

Michael Pledge spent over 20 years in various senior financial positions within PR consultancies. Now a freelance consultant himself, he says:

> *The need to protect an organisation's intangible assets from outsiders is hardly surprising. A brand's reputation, for example, is the most fragile yet precious intangible any organisation owns. Like a pane of glass, the smallest crack or flaw may damage it irreparably.*

But even though branding agencies, for example, are permitted to enter this inner sanctum, freelance consultants are more often barred until they have won their client's unconditional trust and confidence.

On the other hand, it is interesting that for decades the BBC – one of the world's most revered brands – has entrusted the integrity of its reputation to a large freelance workforce. This workforce includes off-camera personnel as well as the on-screen presenters who personify the BBC brand to audiences worldwide.

One could hardly argue that using freelance professionals has cost the BBC respect. In fact, the vast majority of the British public – and worldwide public, for that matter – wouldn't know and probably don't even care about the size of the BBC's freelance roster. Instead, the organisation has successfully protected and nurtured its brand by ensuring that its freelance talent understands and respects the rules of working for the BBC. Their employment status has been reduced to an irrelevance.

LOSS OF CORPORATE CONTROL AND ACCOUNTABILITY

From our research, it appears that control and accountability can be a source of particular concern when using freelance consultants. Problems might arise because they have not been through the same induction and training as everyone else in the organisation. They may not understand its internal approval systems. They may not conform to the organisation's way of doing things and attempt to enforce their own ideas. They are unlikely to be subject to the same hierarchical control or penalties as their permanent colleagues. All these factors could mean that an organisation's normal checks and balances fail because the freelance consultant is acting outside the normal parameters.

As Michael Pledge notes:

> *Freelance consultants must integrate with your internal systems, which may need to be relatively detailed and complex. If a freelance consultant has been placed by an agency, he or she must also meet the agency's expectations. In other words, freelance consultants need to please all the people all the time, which isn't always possible. So maintaining standards and quality control can demand more investment of your in-house management resources.*

Accountability raises many questions. How can you make the freelance consultant truly accountable? Who is ultimately responsible for the project – the hiring organisation or the freelance consultant? Should any contract with freelance consultants include financial penalties? What long-term accountability should a freelance have for a project's success?

Accountability is a two-way affair. The hiring organisation must take its share of responsibility for any failure and resist the temptation to make the freelance consultant a scapegoat for any organisational deficiencies, such as poor briefing.

There is a risk that a freelance consultant can end up operating in a vacuum, especially when his or her involvement on a project is not accepted by permanent staff – despite edicts from on high. If freelance consultants cannot take hold of the project levers quickly enough, they will not be able to overcome the institutional barriers that may block them from achieving their goals. This erodes their credibility and can prevent them from delivering through no fault of their own.

Remember, however, that much of this risk is mitigated by the fact that many freelance consultants work on the understanding that they are only as good as their last assignment. This conviction – which is integral to the freelance condition – acts as an invaluable quality control mechanism. Among many benefits, it helps to free up management time, optimise cost efficiency and foster innovative thinking.

Indeed, many benefits of using freelance consultants can be traced back to this guiding principle.

Transfer of knowledge to competitors

Freelance consultants, by their very nature, go from one client to another. This means that they can acquire intellectual capital from one company and transfer it to another, in the same way that a bee pollinates flowers. This can be a good thing. After all, most companies can benefit from the knowledge that freelance consultants bring with them. But the pollination process can also pose a risk if it threatens something that is integral to a company's competitive edge.

The key is to identify what knowledge is critical to a company's success and then evaluate the pros and cons of briefing a freelance consultant on it.

Of course, this risk equally applies to permanent staff who move from one company to another. The fact is that safeguarding corporate knowledge is difficult in today's fast-paced and porous business environment. In fact, one could argue that being too protective can be equally damaging to a company's growth prospects.

POOR UNDERSTANDING OF THE HIRING ORGANISATION'S BUSINESS

There is a risk that although highly qualified with a good reputation, a freelance consultant may be unable to understand the hiring organisation's business quickly enough to deliver results. This can be highly frustrating for freelance consultant and client alike.

Although unusual, this problem can arise if the project or the nature of the business is so complex or unique that there is nothing to compare them with. To counter the risk, the hirer should recognise that complex projects undertaken by complex organisations demand a combination of skills. It is therefore advisable to take a team approach by marrying the internal knowledge of permanent staff with the external skills of a freelance consultant to achieve the desired result.

OVERLOAD ON MANAGEMENT RESOURCES

Managing freelance consultants requires a different style of management, and this can place pressure on existing management resources – especially when an organisation is new to the freelance option. For example, using freelance consultants requires a greater emphasis on contractual negotiations and good objective-setting, rather than on HR processes. By spending time setting up a freelance framework, management risks neglecting its permanent workforce, which could result in resentment and/or instability.

'In a perfect world, I wouldn't use any freelance consultants at all,' states Rachel Lucas, HR Director at London-based public relations consultancy Lexis. 'But they are a fact of life.' In some ways, Rachel considers freelance consultants a necessary evil. 'Once you have been through the process of hiring a permanent member of staff, you can then nurture and shape them according to your long-term strategy and vision,' she says. 'On the other hand, your freelance resources require constant care and attention and the freelance skills you need are always changing. Freelance consultants are not impossible to manage, they just take up more time.'

Such concerns are valid but not insurmountable. In Chapter 7 we examine the most reliable management techniques for getting the best out of freelance consultants while using your existing framework and resources.

UNSETTLED PERMANENT STAFF

Another risk associated with using freelance consultants is the impact they are likely to have on your permanent staff. In an age when change has become a constant, the arrival of a freelance consultant might be perceived among permanent staff as another sign of even more turbulence ahead. Not surprisingly, they may regard the newcomer with suspicion or even resentment. Numerous questions are likely to arise, among them:

- Is the freelance consultant being paid more than me?
- Will he/she be able to deliver?
- Will he/she fit into the organisation and team?
- Will he/she be after my job?
- Will he/she show me up in front of my boss?
- Will he/she take all our secrets to a competitor?
- Will he/she stay the course or be diverted by the offer of a 'real job'?

In our experience, insecurity can begin surprisingly high up the hierarchy. In fact, it is not unusual for the people who actually hire freelance consultants to favour personnel who are less senior or experienced than they are themselves.

There are sound counter-arguments to justify the use of freelance consultants during times of flux. To most members of the freelance community, change is simply an occupational hazard. All freelancers have to deal with it; many positively thrive on it. Their reputations depend on how successfully they are able to keep their heads while all around are losing theirs.

Reassure permanent staff that freelancers are professionals who know that their reputation is everything. They have chosen the freelance way of working and know that they are paid to produce results. You have chosen them for their commitment to professional standards and ethics, and plan to make them one of your trusted advisers – and not a threat.

Although intangible factors such as personal chemistry and team dynamics are virtually impossible to control, transparent communication and thorough planning is vital to integrating freelance talent as smoothly as possible.

This can be a very sensitive issue and when addressing it it is important to take on board the opinions of permanent staff members. Do they perceive freelance consultants as rivals or colleagues, and how do their attitudes impact on a freelance consultant's performance?

Discovering that the newcomer is earning more money is a predictable cause of resentment among those already in a similar role. But resentment is not always down to money. The arrival of a freelance consultant may be seen as a vote of no confidence in your existing team. There may be concerns that you have a secret agenda, and the freelance consultant may also be suspected as a management spy.

Of course, hiring a freelance consultant does not have to create problems and is often valued as a positive development. For example, if your existing staff are overworked, they are more likely to welcome external support. And because freelance consultants are often valued as being objective, permanent staff may use them as a sounding-board to resolve their political and work-related concerns. After all, it is sometimes easier for people to admit they feel insecure at work if they are confiding in someone outside their management hierarchy.

More than once, we came across freelance consultants who were hired by one manager against the wishes of the other managers only to find themselves the innocent victim of somebody else's power struggle. Without sign-in from all those involved on a project, a freelance consultant is bound to struggle and will probably fail – especially if success depends on the performance of people who are pursuing different outcomes. Other freelancers received a warm welcome from everyone on their arrival, only to be ignored for the rest of the assignment. This was seldom the result of malice – simply ignorance about what managing freelance consultants actually entails. An interesting variation on this theme was the tendency among some organisations to stifle freelance consultants through over-management.

INCREASED COSTS

Certainly, freelance consultants can be an expensive mistake if the hiring organisation has not clearly thought through the reasons for hiring them. When weighing costs, do not be tempted to compare a freelance consultant's day rate with the annual salary of permanent staff at a similar level. Almost always, the day rate will be significantly higher. But a straight like-for-like comparison does not take into account the hidden costs or risks of employing someone permanently. Day rates are also subject to the laws of supply and demand, especially if the freelance skills you are buying are particularly scarce.

As a rule of thumb, organisations will find permanent staff cheaper if they can source a guaranteed supply of people who can be trained easily to do routine work in a business environment that is predictable and stable, and where continuity and/or control of intellectual property is paramount.

We explore this issue in detail in Chapters 2 and 6. But here it is worth remembering that the factors which make freelance costs unsustainable are many and varied. For example, they can escalate as a result of time overruns and missed deadlines, or because quality is below expectations. Often problems can arise because projects themselves are not managed properly, so they overlap or even conflict, leading to the use of too many freelance resources. This inevitably raises costs and decreases efficiency. Effective planning of people resources – both freelance and permanent – is critical to ensuring that you control costs and create value.

Today's world, however, is rarely shaped so perfectly. Increasingly, organisations are learning to accept that there is a price to be paid for flexibility and avoiding the risks and costs of employing people permanently. In other words, freelance consultants often justify higher costs – provided they are properly managed.

COMPROMISED CLIENT RELATIONSHIPS

'To many clients of PR consultancies, permanent staff represent the reassuring combination of quality and continuity that they are happy to pay for,' says freelance consultant Michael Pledge. 'And clients do not always feel comfortable with entrusting their business affairs to freelance consultants. It's often a question of loyalty and trust. A client's insecurities might be largely a question of perception, but those perceptions pay the PR consultancies' bills.'

This resistance to freelance consultants is particularly evident at those critical points where personal relationships are fundamental to the client and supplier relationship. Building the honesty, trust and loyalty that defines these critical bonds is a long-term project even when the personal chemistry works. Expecting a freelance consultant to succeed where many permanent employees might fear to tread jeopardises an equilibrium that can be very delicate. So although freelance consultants often play an indispensable role in-house, many organisations choose not to use them as external ambassadors to their clients.

Rachel Lucas states the case strongly: 'There may come a time,' she says, 'when we consider placing a freelance consultant in a client-facing role. But I can't say when that might be.'

LACK OF COMMITMENT

Cowboy builders are not the only people who juggle multiple clients. If your freelance consultant cannot balance the workload, you are likely to be the loser. Realistically, managing competing demands for their time is an occupational hazard in the freelance community. But, inevitably, some freelance consultants are better at it than others. This problem is less likely to arise where you have booked a client full-time for an agreed period. But even then, a freelance consultant may have to start juggling once the end of the contract is in sight. At this point there is a risk that securing the next assignment might take precedence over your project. Either way, the freelance consultant's service levels might drop, jeopardising your project and even your reputation.

There are several ways to avoid becoming just another client, and many of the best solutions are based on trust. Be upfront and ask your freelance consultants whether they need to juggle other clients. Be honest about the level of commitment you expect from them and get their assurance that they can deliver.

CONCLUSION

Ultimately, you are in the best position to judge whether the benefits of taking on a freelance consultant outweigh the possible risks. If you are not able to protect yourself from the sort of risks we have overviewed in this chapter, do not hire. Instead, resource your project with permanent employees or outsource it completely to an external organisation. But whichever choice you make, each will carry a certain level of risk.

Key point summary

While using freelance consultants brings many advantages, be aware that they can also bring risks such as:

- loss of corporate memory
- dilution of corporate brand, value and culture

- loss of corporate control and accountability
- transfer of knowledge to competitors
- poor understanding of the hiring organisation's business
- overload on management resources
- unsettled permanent staff
- increased costs
- compromised client relationships
- lack of commitment.

4

Deciding when to use a freelance consultant

INTRODUCTION

Deciding whether or not to hire a freelance consultant depends on such a broad spectrum of variables that attempting to present a tick-list of universally applicable criteria would be neither practical nor helpful. At the same time, it is possible to identify generic factors supporting the argument for using the freelance model. After all, the forces of globalisation are such that organisations which once inhabited different worlds now find themselves facing similar challenges. (Managers from oil multinationals and those from campaigning environmental charities, for example, probably share more challenges than they might like to acknowledge.) In this chapter we consider when hiring freelance support is a viable option.

When you should not use freelance consultants

Whereas freelance consultants are the ideal option in certain situations, they may not suit others. You may be better advised to consider alternative options if:

- your business levels – and therefore your required staffing levels – are stable and predictable
- you need continuity and control at all times
- you need to keep corporate intellectual property in-house
- you can easily train staff to undertake ongoing routine work or you have to invest in a high level of training over a long period of time to work efficiently
- you already have a reliable supply of people with the skills you require.

SCENARIO 1: WHEN YOU REQUIRE SPECIALIST SKILLS

Hiring freelance consultants is the most effective way to minimise fixed payroll costs while optimising access to specialist skills as and when they are required.

Commenting on the importance of securing reliable access to specialist skills, Professor Richard Scase, Professor of Organisational Behaviour at the University of Kent at Canterbury, says:

In a global marketplace, what sells today will not necessarily sell tomorrow. Which means that every business must re-invent itself continuously, working quickly to innovate and produce. In practice, the one strength that distinguishes a business from its competitors is talent. And because the most talented people are so often freelance, businesses have no choice but to use them.

Using football as an analogy, Professor Scase suggests that the *galactico* (or big star) principle pioneered by Spanish club Real Madrid has a vital part to play beyond the football pitch.

Once your business has established its brand and reached a critical mass in its development, freelance specialists can provide the injection of energy and skill needed to raise your game to the next level.

CASE STUDY 1: WHEN YOU REQUIRE SPECIALIST SKILLS

Iain Starkey-Smith, Managing Director, Atos Consulting UK

Atos Consulting UK is the UK business consultancy arm of Atos Origin, a leading international IT services company with revenues of over €5 billion and 47,000 staff worldwide, of which around 20 per cent are hired on a freelance basis. It refers to its freelance consultants as 'contractors' and/or 'associates' – particularly when presenting them to clients. Typically senior specialists, associates are hired to complement in-house teams with specialist skills that Atos does not require on a permanent basis.

Atos's current freelance strategy dates back to 2003, when the company moved from depending on in-house staff towards building up a flexible, external talent pool. This move, says Managing Director Iain Starkey-Smith, gave Atos the flexibility to switch the supply of freelance support on and off more easily, eliminating the need for painful redundancies.

As Iain says: 'We take care to ensure that our associates don't manage a contract, but have a senior role on it – ensuring that we retain the intellectual property. Since we are taking the risk, it also makes sense for us to retain the fee income as well as the control. It's a cost-effective solution, and we make a good margin from it.'

Significantly, Atos also has robust debriefing procedures. These enable the company to transfer expertise from external specialists to enrich its internal knowledge bank.

Says Iain: 'It is important that we make sure each associate is fully trained and understands our quality processes. We tend to tailor training according to the individual and the project. If the project is short, training is not appropriate. A basic training programme comprises a half-day to a day covering the delivery assurances that associates must follow. This is followed by two to four days covering the core skills associates require to speak the Atos language and follow our key methodologies while acting as a consultant.'

Associates, notes Iain, are managed in the same way as Atos manages its permanent staff. But although they may be invited to corporate events, they are not subjected to the entire HR process. 'They must learn to be like chameleons – fitting in with Atos and our clients at the same time,' he notes.

'Overall, I would say that using associates is very healthy for a company. You are bringing in new people with different viewpoints and backgrounds, new ideas and understandings. They often have links to universities, which can be very useful. We would be foolish not to expose ourselves to these diverse influences.'

As for evolving their freelance model further, Atos is considering striking a deal with an agency to return all its staff to the job market during quieter periods. At the same time, the company is working on a new business incentive scheme that encourages associates to involve Atos in any new contracts they secure.

'We will certainly continue to use associates for the foreseeable future,' concludes Iain. 'Obviously, we would review the strategy if there was a major crisis. But for our business model, it makes sense.'

CASE STUDY 2: WHEN YOU REQUIRE SPECIALIST SKILLS

Dominic Mills, Editorial Director, Haymarket

Haymarket is a specialist publishing company operating in many of the world's major markets. It is the largest private magazine publisher in the United Kingdom, producing titles published in 23 languages across almost 100 countries.

Using freelancers is strongly established in the publishing sector, and is by no means the novel phenomenon it is in some business areas. Haymarket Publishing in the UK is certainly reliant on freelancers: 5 to 10 per cent of its 300-strong editorial team is freelance. Writing articles is so specifically project-based that it lends itself extremely well to the freelance model because there is a definite beginning and end rather than an ongoing general need.

According to Dominic Mills, Haymarket's Editorial Director: 'Like any publishing house, we have a steady roster of freelancers that we call on to write articles, usually when we need specialists from a particular area who really know their field inside out. Freelancers often have a ready-made network of contacts they can use to comment on the article. What's more, they are generally up to speed on the latest developments in their field.

'A more generalist journalist working for a title on a permanent basis would find a very specialist subject more difficult. Additionally, in a fast-paced environment with constant deadlines such as ours, using freelancers means we have more flexibility.'

Going freelance is a well-trodden career path among journalists. In fact, most freelancers on Haymarket's roster are ex-Haymarket employees who still do much of their writing for the company. 'This means that we have some excellent relationships with our freelancers and consider them to be part of the extended family,' comments Dominic.

'Generally, Haymarket's experience of using freelancers has been positive. Without them, we would find it difficult to operate efficiently.'

CASE STUDY 3: WHEN YOU REQUIRE SPECIALIST SKILLS

Fiona Stephens, Business Change Manager, Transforming HR Programme, DEFRA

'We use freelance consultants when we need to bring in a specific skill set. For example, technical knowledge. In fact, the need for specific skills is perhaps the most common reason for using freelance consultants across the whole public sector.

'Incidentally, in our programme we call them "contractors" or "consultants", and they mainly have IT skills. But some of the contractors take real offence if you call them consultants.

'Recently, we have become more skilful at identifying the core skills we already have on the payroll and those we need to bring in on a freelance basis.

'Because DEFRA is moving towards keeping control of its own business, responsibility for our freelance resources lies with the line management chain, rather than HR. If a line manager decides they have a requirement for a freelance consultant, they submit a business case, which in my case is to my programme manager for approval. The business case will list the reasons for hiring, value-for-money criteria and what skill sets are required. If approved, a purchase order is raised and monitored by our financial system.

'We are obliged to advertise permanent roles internally and because of the restructuring across the Civil Service and the need to spend public funds wisely, we would always look carefully at what internal resource is available – even for short-term roles. Once we have established the business case for a freelance role, we would tend to use agencies rather than advertising to find us the right person.

'We bring in freelance consultants for a set time to produce a particular output. Their contracts can be extended if there is a business case to do so. Once hired, freelance consultants become key members of the team. There is no 'us and them' and working relationships are good. Although freelance consultants are paid significantly more than permanent staff, permanent staff generally understand why this happens. Unlike freelance consultants, permanent staff are not subject to the same job insecurity, for example. Nor do freelancers receive any additional benefits.

'Freelance consultants are given enough background and strategic information to put the project in context, but we don't give them the same level of information as we give our permanent staff. We don't give them much information on the organisation because they are generally not interested in receiving it. We tend to set the level of information they receive according to how much they need to deliver their project. Although they all have access to the intranet and can easily find any information they require.

'In my area, freelance consultants attend weekly and quarterly team meetings, but they are not covered by any HR process. We carefully monitor their outputs, but expect them to manage themselves, and give them contact points to discuss any issues that may arise. If someone is not up to scratch, we get rid of them quickly.

'Looking ahead, there are various developments that may reduce our dependency on external people. For example, Senior Civil Servants are now expected to move between delivery, policy and corporate areas as well as having experience of other sectors. Eventually this policy will be extended to all levels of the Civil Service. The aim is to raise the calibre of internal staff, making them more rounded operators. At the same time, the public sector is improving the way it transfers skills by, for example, using freelance consultants to train up permanent staff.'

SCENARIO 2: WHEN CHANGE BECOMES A CONSTANT

In recent years, the PR industry has changed so radically that we no longer have a choice. Freelance consultants are a fact of business life.

Rachel Lucas, HR Director, Lexis Public Relations

The freelance option is tried and tested among organisations that require experienced change specialists to guide them through a period of change, then select the permanent employees who will succeed them once the change programme is complete. Many of the most experienced specialists in this particular area call themselves 'interim managers', a term that we examine in Chapter 1 (see pages 5–8).

Marketing specialist Janet Morris became an interim manager following a series of permanent positions, many in the aviation sector. She argues that people with her skills and mindset make ideal partners for organisations confronting the challenges of internal change. She applies her argument to the private and public sector alike.

'Our credibility as interim managers depends on how effectively we handle change,' she says. 'The most successful interim managers positively thrive on it. This means they are able to bring the confidence and clarity required to guide permanent staff through periods of upheaval and transformation.'

Since change has become a constant for so many organisations in the global age, Janet predicts a long-term demand for interim managers.

Her view is shared by Rachel Lucas, HR Director at London-based public relations consultancy, Lexis. She also puts the ascendancy of freelance consultants down to the C-word. 'In recent years,' says Rachel, 'the PR industry has changed so radically that we no longer have a choice. Freelance consultants are a fact of business life.'

'Call it the Jamie Oliver effect,' she says. 'In the past, we have arrived at work to find him all over the front pages with his latest campaign. Overnight, he had hijacked the news agenda and we had no choice but to abandon our carefully laid plans and follow him.'

Clearly, when the unpredictable becomes the rule rather than the exception and flexibility is of the essence, freelance consultants are often a strong option.

CASE STUDY 1: WHEN CHANGE BECOMES A CONSTANT

Nick Robeson, Chief Executive, Boyden Interim Management Limited

A large UK service provider in the telecommunications field with a turnover of approximately £100 million and 450 employees required an interim business development director.

'The business was going through a great deal of change. Following the sale of the business and subsequent purchase by another group, most senior management left as a result of the acquisition and the overall uncertainty surrounding the future strategy of the parent company for this business.

'Our client briefed the interim business development director to integrate the roles of three sales directors and 100 personnel, and to stabilise the infrastructure and competencies for selling services via direct, vertical market, business, residential and resale channels.

'Our interim achieved year-on-year revenue growth across all channels to market and the restructuring and downsizing of the commercial sales channel. Productivity was improved, and return on investment. Product specialists were introduced in order to accelerate diversification and overall margins, and compensation was aligned to revenues, not order intake. Personally, he also secured a contract with minimum first-year revenues of £12 million and negotiated a joint venture to re-establish the business' university sector market leadership.'

SCENARIO 3: WHEN YOUR ORGANISATION IS GROWING

During periods of rapid expansion, when an organisation needs to staff up quickly, bringing in seasoned freelance professionals makes good sense. Not only can they master the brief with minimum delay, but they need minimal management to execute it.

Geoff Nicol – Managing Director of the strategic communications group Navyblue – is a persuasive exponent of the argument that freelance consultants can be an important factor in managing the organic growth of a company – provided they are handled with care.

Most growing companies inevitably experience the classic Catch-22: you need more staff before taking on new clients, but you need more clients before you can take on more staff. Using freelance consultants can give you the flexibility you need to manage the peaks and troughs until you achieve the critical balance between workflow and headcount.

CASE STUDY 1: WHEN YOUR ORGANISATION IS GROWING

Jennie Talman and Emma Crozier Co-founders, Just Health Public Relations Ltd

'Just' is a specialist health public relations consultancy that has recently opened its doors to work with pharmaceutical companies and fmcg companies who have brands with a health message. It intends to grow by supplementing its nucleus of permanent staff with a network of freelance consultants.

'We made a decision from the very beginning that we would partner with freelance consultants to help grow the business,' says co-founder, Jennie Talman. 'This is especially important during the first year while the business is being established and demand can be unpredictable. The last thing we want to do is say "No" to a client who wants to work with us. Using freelancers is very established in the healthcare world so our clients will be comfortable with this route.'

'Then as the business grows up, we will ensure that there is a balance between permanent staff and freelance consultants but due to talent shortages, freelancers will always be crucial to our business model. It can take a long time to find the right person to join the team permanently so freelancers effectively fill the gap. It can also be a clever way to test a potential new recruit by asking them to freelance for you first.

'We also use freelance consultants to provide extended cover – for example, maternity leave – to help when the volume of work escalates, to participate in new business pitches and to add specialist skills.'

Emma Crozier, co-founder, suggests several reasons for their decision. 'Firstly, using freelancers means that we don't have to make a long-term commitment and will enable us to keep a tight control over employment costs. This means we only pay for people's time when there is a higher volume of work. When it's quieter, we use our freelancers less. Secondly, we can hire at short notice, which is so important in our business when we can win a project and need to start working on the client's business straight away. Finally, it is a simpler and quicker way to get people onto headcount. We're not burdened with excess administration.'

The benefits are substantial. 'Increased productivity is the primary one,' says Emma. 'For example, we may only have enough work to fill someone's time for part of a week. This is difficult to do with permanent staff who need to be fully utilised, but it is perfect for a freelancer. Using a mix of freelance and permanent staff ensures that we get our utilisation rates right, and ultimately this enhances profitability.

In Emma's experience, freelance consultants are very conscientious and work hard. If they do not deliver, they risk compromising their reputations. They can also spread best practice as a result of their broad experience, transferring skills and knowledge.

'Working with freelancers is uncomplicated as long as you bring in people who match your culture and you get the initial briefing right, so you need to be clear on why you are bringing

CASE STUDY continued

them in, and permanent staff understand why they are needed. If your relationship is set up right, then it all runs itself and doesn't require much intervention by management, beyond checking periodically that they are still on brief.'

In the final analysis, Jennie has found that hiring freelance consultants is a sensible way to grow a business. As she says: 'Managing costs is crucial for a small business – especially in its first year. And it is good for the company, keeping the culture fresh and contributing to an interesting and dynamic workplace.'

CASE STUDY 2: WHEN YOUR ORGANISATION IS GROWING

Antoine Lever, Commercial Director, Omniis Limited

Omniis provides IT solutions including remote IT support, document management and VoIP telephony. Established three years ago, the company employs 12 people. Its Commercial Director, Antoine Lever, explains why Omniis decided to use freelance consultants.

'There were three main reasons. First, to fill gaps in our own resourcing capacity, so that we can manage peaks and troughs in our business. Secondly, to supplement skills that we don't have in-house. Thirdly, to give us access to the senior strategic advice we cannot afford to employ full-time in support areas including HR, legal affairs, accountancy, and marketing, as well as our non-executive directors.'

At any one time, Antoine estimates, there may be up to 10 freelance consultants involved with Omniis. 'As a small business, we find it difficult to find really good people. So if we decide that we want to make a permanent hire, we often have no choice but to use freelance consultants while we conduct our search.'

Primarily, Omniis chooses highly skilled and highly experienced freelance consultants. 'That's because we need them to be client-facing,' explains Antoine. 'Given the calibre of the people we hire, we invariably learn something from them.'

SCENARIO 4: WHEN YOU'D PREFER TO TRY BEFORE YOU BUY

There are plenty of freelance consultants who are not in the market for a permanent job. On the other hand, there are some who use freelance consulting to 'test drive' a mix of working environments before committing to a permanent position with the one that suits them best. This process works both ways. For organisations in many sectors, 'trying before you buy' is the accepted way of selecting permanent staff.

Indeed, successfully hiring people on a freelance basis can open the door to establishing a more permanent relationship with them. If people prove their value to your organisation as freelance consultants, they are likely to add even more value should they choose to go on the books – although they may well expect to see flexible working options written into their permanent contract. As an employer, you will need to be sure that they have the mindset and attitude to cope with a permanent position.

Working in a freelance capacity gives people an opportunity to find their place in your organisation and its culture while developing their internal contacts and networks. This familiarisation period gives both you and the freelance consultant an opportunity to assess the best way to harness his or her talents.

The opposite also applies. Hiring someone as a freelance consultant before taking him or her on permanently reduces the risk of employing someone unsuitable. This in turn eliminates recruitment and redundancy costs as well as frustration and wasted time.

CASE STUDY 1: WHEN YOU'D PREFER TO TRY BEFORE YOU BUY

Nick Southgate, Creative Director, Ricochet

Traditionally, freelancing is the dominant employment model in the TV industry, and the 'try before you buy' principle is increasingly important to the relationship between organisations and the freelance consultants they hire.

As Nick Southgate, Creative Director at Brighton-based TV production company Ricochet, says: 'This industry could not function without freelancers. It would be a disaster. Having an army of permanent employees on the books would be financial suicide for companies, especially small ones. Business fluctuates so widely and forecasting is very difficult. You are constantly scaling up and down. We might have three projects on the go at any one time, or 15. It all depends on the broadcasters and ratings.'

That's not to say that the permanent model has no place in the TV industry. But according to Nick, having permanent employees in a TV company is a relatively new concept, and impossible when companies are small. All new staff join Ricochet as fixed-term employees, in line with the 'try before you buy' process. If freelance consultants prove their worth, they are passed from project to project internally – and may be offered a staff position. 'Frankly, we don't care if someone is permanent or freelance. It's their talent that counts.'

SCENARIO 5: WHEN YOU REQUIRE EXTENDED COVER

In any organisation, staffing levels can be significantly reduced when permanent employees take maternity leave, sick leave, study leave, training leave, holidays, sabbaticals – and so on. Some absences are more predictable and finite than others, which makes planning relatively straightforward. But even the most rigorous schedulers cannot always conjure up the right people with the right skills at the right time.

Not surprisingly, perhaps, more organisations are turning to the freelance market to provide staff cover. We found that many of them are pleasantly surprised by the added value that good freelance consultants bring to an assignment.

CASE STUDY 1: WHEN YOU REQUIRE EXTENDED COVER

Aminata Kamara, HR Officer, Munro & Forster

Munro & Forster (M&F) is an independent communications consultancy. In business for over 20 years, it is among the UK's top 10 health and well-being consultancies, and has four core teams covering the consumer, healthcare, public and voluntary, and political sectors.

Aminata Kamara, M&F's HR Officer, says that the business uses freelance consultants primarily to provide cover. 'That could mean short-term holiday cover, cover to handle higher workloads or longer-term maternity cover. Additionally, if someone permanent is leaving and we cannot find a replacement quickly enough, we will use a freelancer to cover during the interim. Occasionally, we use freelancers to help on new business proposals.'

According to Aminata, the speed with which freelance consultants settle into their role is another sound reason for hiring them. 'We work very closely with two freelance resourcing agencies. Because they know our business inside out, they are able to supply talented consultants at very short notice. The people they send us are used to adapting to new situations and getting up to speed very quickly. That means they are productive and useful to our organisation from the start. We always hire people on a one-week trial so that if things don't work out for any reason, we're not tied into keeping them.'

In Aminata's experience, using freelance consultants is very positive. 'It offers us the ultimate in flexibility when we don't have time to plan ahead.'

CASE STUDY 2: WHEN YOU REQUIRE EXTENDED COVER

Shirley Cramer, Chief Executive, Dyslexia Institute

The Dyslexia Institute is an educational charity founded in 1972 to assess and teach people with dyslexia, and to train teachers. It employs over 250 staff, including 70 educational psychologists.

Shirley Cramer, Chief Executive at the Dyslexia Institute, argues that freelance consultants hired to cover for permanent staff invariably enrich an organisation with their own skills and experience. What's more, their expertise is often easily transferable from one project to another, which helps to reinforce an organisation's existing capabilities.

'When our communication team hired a freelance consultant for maternity cover,' recalls Shirley, 'we chose someone with a specific skill, which meant we could also use her on a branding project. In another case, we brought in a freelance consultant to provide long-term sick leave cover. We didn't know how long our permanent team member would be signed-off for. But we were able to select a freelance replacement with the skills to handle the workload, bring in an external perspective – and keep out of office politics.'

In both cases, says Shirley, the original contract has been extended to provide the communications team with ongoing cover. 'Crucially, the freelance consultants involved have helped to enhance our in-house knowledge bank by providing skills that our permanent team lacked. Using freelancers in the communications team is a relatively new departure for us. But so far, it has certainly exceeded my expectations and benefited the organisation tremendously.'

SCENARIO 6: WHEN YOU NEED TO HANDLE PEAKS AND TROUGHS

Peaks and troughs have long been a feature of working life for many. In seasonal sectors – agriculture, hospitality and tourism, to name just three – they are the rule rather than the exception. But globalisation has compressed the space between them and made them deeper, steeper and more treacherous to navigate. Freelance consultants bring the skills, flexibility and cost-efficiencies required to minimise the resulting turbulence.

CASE STUDY 1: WHEN YOU NEED TO HANDLE PEAKS AND TROUGHS

The HR Director of a leading event marketing consultancy

The respondent is HR Director of a leading event marketing consultancy with global expertise in trade shows and conferences through to roadshows, mobile marketing and sponsorships.

The business has always drawn on freelance support across all its operations. But 18 months ago a strategic decision was taken to use freelance consultants to help grow the business.

The HR Director explains: 'At any one time, we could have 20 freelancers in the business and 75 permanent staff. The event industry fluctuates tremendously and while we take every care to forecast the expected volume of activity, there are times when work drops away or events move dates. The unpredictable has an impact on our staffing levels.

'We responded by taking a decision to match our permanent headcount to the lowest threshold of work that we could function with. We then "staff up" with freelancers whenever we experience peaks in our workload. This gives us tighter control and greater financial benefits because we only use staff as and when the work is there.'

The company prefers to maintain a core of high-quality freelancers that it can call on at any time throughout the year. Not only are the core freelance consultants loyal, they also know the business inside out, cutting time required for training and ensuring that freelance consultants quickly become as productive as permanent staff.

'Using freelancers also means that we can hire higher skills levels and concentrate on specific skill bases,' says the HR Director. 'For example, if we need a producer with experience of large-scale conferences or international experience to work on events abroad, we can find a career freelancer who specialises in that particular area.'

The HR Director discerns just one disadvantage of using such a high number of freelance

CASE STUDY continued

consultants: 'There is a danger they could learn a lot from us, then use that knowledge to benefit their other clients – our competitors. There is also the danger that they could build up a relationship with our clients and take a permanent job or freelance assignment with them.

'We manage this area very carefully and try to limit direct contact between our freelance consultants and our clients. But there is only so much we can do to prevent it. Ultimately, it comes down to trust. Fortunately, we feel we've built up a huge amount of loyalty with our team of freelancers.'

CASE STUDY 2: WHEN YOU NEED TO HANDLE PEAKS AND TROUGHS

Fiona Dent, Director of Faculty Development, Ashridge Management College

Executives attending any reputable business school must rank among the most challenging students to face any teacher. Yet Ashridge Management College – ranked by the *Financial Times* as one of the world's top 30 executive education institutions – has no hesitation about using 'associates', the term it uses to define its freelance teachers.

'To be frank,' says Fiona Dent, Ashridge's Director of Faculty Development, 'standing before one of our classes can be a bruising experience. Our students take no prisoners and our clients soon let us know if we fall below standard. Teaching here is rather like being an actor – you're only as good as your last performance. If an associate doesn't perform well enough, we don't ask them back.'

Despite the potential risks, associates have become an integral part of the Ashridge way. Indeed, around 50 per cent of current Faculty members are non-permanent. 'The college will always have a core of permanent staff, but we could never meet market demand without associates,' explains Fiona. 'For a start, they give us the flexibility to manage peaks and troughs in demand.

'While helping us to meet our long-term needs cost-effectively, our associates are also a reliable source of one-off specialist skills. And, of course, they keep us fresh.' In fact, Ashridge values its associates so highly that it actively encourages its permanent teaching staff to combine their full-time roles with freelance assignments.

'We seem to have struck a sound balance between the permanent model and the freelance model,' says Fiona. 'Associates value the freedom of freelancing but also identify strongly with Ashridge and what it stands for. The next challenge is to continue to develop the way we manage them. Among other things, this means integrating them even more closely into day-to-day affairs, making them feel part of the team.'

Fiona emphasises that managing Ashridge's associates correctly demands significant time and energy. 'Ultimately, however, our relationship with them is based on trust. In fact, we don't even ask them to sign formal contracts. Instead, we have an associates' charter, outlining what we expect from them – and what they can expect from us.'

CASE STUDY 3: WHEN YOU NEED TO HANDLE PEAKS AND TROUGHS

The consultancy argument – Michael Pledge, Freelance Finance Director

Once upon a time, most clients would engage consultancies on a retainer basis. Now, however, clients tend to commission work on a project basis. Among other challenges, this has made it more difficult for suppliers to plan their human resourcing requirements. In addition, the nature of the projects they work on is also becoming more difficult to predict. Once again, optimum flexibility is essential, especially because high-pressure projects are typically interspersed with relatively quiet periods. In these circumstances, hiring freelance consultants is a proven option among consultancies – especially when controlling costs is a priority.

Michael Pledge spent over 20 years in various senior financial positions within PR consultancies. In 1980, he joined the Ogilvy Group before moving to Burson-Marsteller, then Hill & Knowlton, at that time the UK's biggest PR consultancy with a turnover of £40 million.

His extensive experience of PR and advertising consultancies has given him a unique insight into the financial viability of using freelance consultants. Michael acknowledges that the freelance option offers many distinct advantages. 'It helps consultancies deal with the peaks and troughs. It helps to supplement the in-house skill base. It can dramatically reduce office overheads. But ultimately I would argue that the most compelling reason for using freelance consultants is financial transparency.'

As Michael points out, 'An average consultancy might expect someone on the payroll to log an average of 28 hours of billable time per week – time which can be charged to the client. Very few of them hit that target. If a manager asks a permanent staff member to complete a task in 10 hours, experience demonstrates they will take 15 hours over it and a client cannot be charged for the five hours of over-servicing.

'On the other hand,' continues Michael, 'once a freelance consultant has agreed to do a job in 10 hours for a given price, that's it. Your fixed costs are minimised and you have no hidden costs to account for. What's more, once the assignment is over, you are not obliged to keep the freelance consultant gainfully employed with other tasks.'

This degree of transparency delivers a cost-efficiency that is particularly important at a time when consultancies need to replace up to a third of existing business every year. 'There is no doubt,' concludes Michael, 'that freelance consultants can be a very strong card in any organisation's hand. The trick is to play them skilfully, so that you sustain the reassuring combination of continuity and quality that clients usually associate with permanent staff.'

SCENARIO 7: WHEN YOU ARE FACING A SKILLS SHORTAGE

The scarcity of skills in the labour market is endemic in some sectors and is likely to intensify across many others. For some organisations, hiring freelance consultants offers a reliable and cost-effective route to the specialised skills they require. Other organisations – notably those in the IT sector – simply have no choice but to hire freelance consultants. Not surprisingly, a growing number of specialists are cashing in on the growing demand for their expertise by going freelance.

CASE STUDY 1: WHEN YOU ARE FACING A SKILLS SHORTAGE

An HR Manager in a Group of communications companies, UK

One well-established UK Group comprises specialist communications companies across a wide range of disciplines. The Group has around 1,000 employees.

'As a consultancy we can't live without our freelancers,' says its HR Manager. 'They're an essential part of everyday business. Our creative teams don't even use the terms "freelance" or "permanent" because freelancers are such an integral part of the organisation. A person's employment status no longer seems as important as it once did.'

'The Group has always used freelancers,' continues the Manager. 'But the volume has risen significantly over the past year for a number of reasons. For a start, business has grown rapidly and using freelancers has provided us with a flexible solution for managing additional work. Another reason for using freelancers is to avoid permanent headcount issues, but primarily we use them because of the skills shortage within the sectors we operate in.'

The Group needs an extremely wide range of people with specialist skills. They range from experts who are amazingly creative on Apple Macs to others with highly specialised technical skills, such as information architects. Other rare talents include account managers and finance professionals with broader all-round experience.

Says the Manager: 'It's becoming more and more difficult to find people with the specialist skills we need on a permanent basis. Additionally, once permanent people within our consultancy realise that freelancers get a much higher day rate, they often make the transition to freelancing. This makes retaining good people on a permanent basis even more difficult. This is especially true among creative personnel, where freelancing has been commonplace for many years now.

'But it also applies to account managers, who know they're in demand. We find it difficult getting them to commit because they have the pick of the roles. It means we have to offer some pretty good packages to get people to stay with us permanently.'

Weighing up the advantages of using freelance consultants, the HR Manager says: 'You can be precise about what you need, so you don't have to hire generalists unnecessarily. It also enables us to monitor our costs and keep track of how long someone has been with us. When there's no longer a huge volume of work, you can very simply tell freelance consultants on short-term assignments that their services are no longer required.'

CASE STUDY 2: WHEN YOU ARE FACING A SKILLS SHORTAGE

Shirley Cramer, Chief Executive, Dyslexia Institute

The Dyslexia Institute is an educational charity, founded in 1972 to assess and teach people with dyslexia and to train teachers. It employs over 250 staff and 70 educational psychologists, who are employed on a freelance basis. They work independently – many have their own businesses – and are located around the UK. According to Shirley Cramer, the institute's director, 'They are the best people in their field. They have made the choice to go independent – and we would struggle to retain them on a permanent basis.

'The freelance option works for both parties, meeting everyone's needs. The psychologists get training and equipment they might have difficulty accessing without us. We get access to some great, flexible talent that we can use as and when we need it.

'As a charity with limited budgets, using freelancers also means that we can get the kind of person we would like on a permanent basis, but can't afford to employ on a permanent or full-time contract.'

SCENARIO 8: WHEN INCREASING YOUR PERMANENT HEADCOUNT BECOMES AN ISSUE

For many managers, the struggle to operate efficiently without increasing their permanent headcount has become a fact of working life. Hiring freelance consultants to meet this challenge has become equally commonplace. With pressure on staffing budgets unlikely to ease, the use of freelance consultants is likely to increase. Not only do they deliver specific skills cost-effectively, but in many cases they can be placed in post far more quickly than a permanent employee.

CASE STUDY 1: WHEN INCREASING YOUR PERMANENT HEADCOUNT BECOMES AN ISSUE

An Editor in a Government Department

'When I joined the Department,' says one of the Department Editors, 'I inherited a situation where our funding had been cut following a recent restructure. Permanent headcount issues were key and bringing in freelancers helped to resolve them. Because freelancers don't represent a fixed cost, hiring them gave us control over our finances while providing the specialist skills and workload assistance we desperately needed.'

The Editor also found that freelance consultants brought additional benefits. 'For a start, they have a much better sense of the marketplace. Working for different clients means they need to keep up to date with developments. This proved especially important when we were looking for people with specialist skills – such as web programming.'

CASE STUDY continued

On the downside, the Editor is conscious that his current editorial team is freelance. 'As a result, I don't have the security of having a permanent team member who is going to stay longer-term. This means we have to spend more time than we would like on retraining, and periods of higher staff turnover are unsettling. Overall, however, using freelancers does provide us with an effective solution to our headcount issues.'

CASE STUDY 2: WHEN INCREASING YOUR PERMANENT HEADCOUNT BECOMES AN ISSUE

Nick Robeson, Chief Executive, Boyden Interim Management Limited

The UK subsidiary of a market leader in the global document market had an urgent requirement for an interim manager following the sudden departure of its IT Director.

'During the first three months of the assignment the parent company imposed a recruitment freeze and asked the interim manager to stay on until it was lifted and a successor could be found.

'The interim manager then had to provide strategic technical direction since the urgent need to initiate an Internet/e-business programme arose. The marketing department had initially been responsible for Internet, but as e-business emerged the Internet systems required close integration within the operational IT systems. A few months later the recruitment freeze was lifted and a successor appointed within two months.

'While the freeze was in place it gave the interim manager ample opportunity to scope the role for the incoming director of IT. Not only did this help the headhunters involved but it increased the likelihood that the incumbent would stay for a longer period of time because the scope to grow within the role was much greater.'

SCENARIO 9: WHEN YOU REQUIRE AN INJECTION OF NEW IDEAS AND APPROACHES

Innovation is the currency of the future, and freelance consultants can act as an indispensable source of creative energy and new ideas. Their objectivity can also be very useful when it comes to refreshing your organisation with new approaches and fresh perspectives.

CASE STUDY 1: WHEN YOU REQUIRE AN INJECTION OF NEW IDEAS AND APPROACHES

Vanessa Wright, Communications Director, Chivas Brothers

Chivas Brothers was established by Pernod Ricard as the Group's Scotch whisky business in December 2001, following its acquisition of Seagram. Subsequently, Pernod Ricard acquired Allied Domecq, making it the world's second biggest drinks, wine and spirits company.

Chivas Brothers now has approximately 2,000 employees and 30 sites in the UK, including distilleries. Its key brands include Chivas Regal, Ballantine's, The Glenlivet, Royal Salute, Clan Campbell and Beefeater Gin.

As Communications Director, Vanessa Wright has used a number of freelance consultants for a variety of reasons. 'One of my most memorable and useful hires', she recalls, 'was a senior interim manager we brought on board to fulfil a strategic brainstorm role so we could review our approach. He came in for a two-day brainstorm offsite with the entire communications team, during which he led a review of our communications plan for the forthcoming year.'

'However senior you are, there is always more you can learn. Bringing in an independent adviser was a very positive experience. We all learned from the exercise – it enabled us to work together more closely and meant that the project was really owned by the whole team.'

As Vanessa comments, receiving independent advice from an adviser with an external perspective is invaluable. 'Working with someone who is the best in their class meant that our original plan was challenged, and together we formulated some great ideas to take us forward over the year.'

Vanessa warns that some senior managers may be uncomfortable with the idea of bringing in an external person. 'But I believe it shows you are confident in your position, and understand that you can learn a great deal from someone who has many years' experience in their specialist field,' she notes.

SCENARIO 10: WHEN YOU HAVE A CRISIS TO MANAGE

Unsurprisingly, it is common practice for organisations to involve freelance consultants in times of crisis. Of course, crises can strike any part of an organisation, confounding even the most meticulous prevention systems. Whatever their symptoms, tackling the causes inevitably demands a high level of specialist expertise at short notice for a finite period. The freelance option gives organisations the flexibility to fulfil all these requirements with absolute precision. Another advantage of using freelance consultants in a crisis is that an organisation can release them once the problem is resolved, the post-mortem is over and the lessons have been listed.

CASE STUDY 1: WHEN YOU HAVE A CRISIS TO MANAGE

Justin Everard, News Manager, Food Standards Agency

The Food Standards Agency (FSA) is an independent Government department set up by an Act of Parliament in 2000 to protect the public's health and consumer interests in relation to food.

'The FSA uses freelancers across its functions, most notably communications. Indeed, freelancers are often used because they provide increased flexibility in our staffing requirements. Generally we use freelancers to provide cover when people leave and during the sometimes lengthy process of resourcing their replacement,' explains Justin Everard, the FSA's News Manager.

'However there have been instances when we've needed freelancers for specific reasons. One example, was when the Sudan 1 incident* broke in February 2005. We had people away on holiday and off sick – but we needed support fast.

'There was an urgent need for experienced people who could manage the situation, had previous exposure to incidents of this sort and would be able to answer questions from journalists. The freelancers we chose had to be able to learn quickly while remaining sensitive to the needs of the organisation and taking direction from their permanent colleagues. We took on three people short-term to manage the initial stages of the incident. Some stayed longer to handle the ongoing, longer-term issues that arose.

'Overall I was really pleased with the individuals who came in to assist,' concludes Justin. 'They were eager to help and fitted in well with the permanent team. Their assistance at a crucial time was invaluable.'

* In February 2005, the British Food Standards Agency issued a recall notice on 350 foods because of the contamination of chilli powder with the potentially cancer-causing substance Sudan 1.

CASE STUDY 2: WHEN YOU HAVE A CRISIS TO MANAGE

Nick Robeson, Chief Executive, Boyden Interim Management Limited

An interim manager was required to assist in the turnaround and sale of a well-known branded product in the paper industry.

'The task ahead was to implement a recovery plan, manage a considerable redundancy programme and outflank the most militant section of the union, persuading the remaining unions and workers to accept new contracts. This was to open the way for the eventual sale of the business.

'The interim finance director selected had extensive experience and the temperament to manage the high-pressure role while having the ability to fit in with the rest of the team.

'His immediate task to avert a crisis was to manage the solvency position and the cash-flow through the development of good relationships with key suppliers and customers and the negotiation of favourable terms. He established regular contact with the bank, increasing confidence as the necessity for funds was gradually reduced through cash management and the sale of assets.

'Then disaster hit again. A new fully integrated planning and scheduling system went live and brought the business to a standstill. The interim finance director assumed control of the project and within three months had solved the problems and regained control of the business.

Finally, he assisted in the strategic planning for the sale of the business, which was duly accomplished with the sale to a UK public group under new management.'

Key point summary

There are various circumstances that favour the use of freelance consultants:

- when you require specialist skills
- when change becomes a constant
- when your organisation is growing
- when you would prefer to try before you buy
- when you require extended cover
- when you need to handle peaks and troughs
- when you are facing a skills shortage
- when increasing your permanent headcount becomes an issue
- when you require an injection of new ideas and approaches
- when you have a crisis to manage.

5

How to find the most suitable freelance consultants

INTRODUCTION

When it comes to resourcing freelance consultants, there are essentially two options: either you can hire them yourself, using a combination of traditional and online tools, or you can appoint a freelance resourcing agency.

Whichever route you choose, it is essential to ensure that resourcing decisions are taken by an executive at senior management level. Delegating this role any further down your organisation can seriously compromise the quality of the freelance consultants you engage. So can making decisions by committee, where lack of speed and the potential for power games can also produce poor decisions. Although the administrative aspects of resourcing can be undertaken at a relatively junior level, speed is always important. If you choose the freelance resourcing agency option, don't brief too many agencies in any one area. Typically, organisations that do so are unclear about the type of person they want to hire and why.

Bear in mind that many of the principles that apply to recruiting permanent staff also apply to hiring freelance consultants. In both cases, finding the best demands time, know-how and resources.

OPTION 1: HIRING FREELANCE CONSULTANTS YOURSELF

Maintaining your own freelance talent pool

- Log the date a CV is received – they date quickly.
- Log the name and personal details, home address, key skills, daily rate, availability.
- Enter the data into a searchable database.
- Assign one person to update the database with new skills/experience, etc.
- Track people's availability, which changes regularly.
- Comply with the data protection legislation.
- Keep freelance consultants informed of your current and future needs.
- Log all post-assignment feedback on freelance consultants.
- Establish administration procedures such as contract-signing, payment procedures, etc.

Using your own resources to identify and hire freelance consultants might seem the cheapest and simplest option. But Geoff Nicol – who heads up the strategic communications group Navyblue – warns against underestimating the effort it takes. 'Using freelance consultants is rarely a simple business,' he notes. 'If you're going to manage your freelance requirements on your own, do it properly – or don't do it all.'

And in Geoff's view, doing it properly goes beyond the essential yet time-consuming business of maintaining a database of freelance consultants. It also means keeping your antenna constantly attuned for new talent. Football is a good example of a global industry that has taken this lesson to heart, so that the most successful football clubs invest heavily in their talent-scouting networks.

One way to follow the football industry's example is by building your own talent bank. If you are able to predict when you are most likely to require freelance support, it makes sense to build up your talent bank with suitable names before demand escalates. Interviewing as many people as possible when workloads are relatively light minimises the risk of discovering that there are no freelance consultants for hire when you need them most.

The fact is that the best freelance consultants are not always available, so take steps to ensure that you always have a second choice if your first choice is busy. This means looking beyond your immediate needs and factoring freelance support into your long-term planning. Consider innovations such as making down-payments on a freelance consultant's time several months in advance. As well as giving freelance consultants an incentive to work for you, this type of forward planning helps you to control your costs.

Networking is also essential to building up your talent bank. It is important to invest as much time and thought in meeting new freelancers as you invest in meeting potential clients. Target venues and events that are most likely to attract the sort of freelance talent you are looking for. If appropriate, consider hosting your own networking evenings.

At every possible opportunity, promote your organisation as the freelance consultant's client of choice. There are three effective ways to achieve this. First, keep freelance consultants in the communication loop. The more you demonstrate your commitment to them, the more they are likely to reciprocate. Which means that when demand for their skills begins to outstrip supply, they are more likely to give you first refusal. Secondly, guarantee your freelance consultants regular work whenever possible, bearing in mind that your control over workflow may be limited. Thirdly, agree to pay the freelance consultant within a specific period. Whether you agree one week, 30 days, or even longer, stick to the agreed timescales. Nothing disillusions a freelance consultant more than having to chase outstanding invoices.

There are various sound reasons organisations might choose to keep the freelance resourcing process in-house. The most obvious is cost: the organisation simply cannot afford to pay an agency. By contrast, other organisations may be confident that their internal resources are capable of managing the hiring process more efficiently than an outside agency. Then there are those organisations that operate in such a specialised niche that it is relatively easy for them to track freelance talent.

If you choose the in-house option, never underestimate the level of communication required to manage a pool of freelance talent effectively. Communication by phone, email or face-to-face contact is essential when briefing freelance consultants on a new assignment, handling any issues or problems that arise during the assignment, or managing any variations that may apply to the original contract as a result of illness or changes in availability, etc. The freelance market is never static, and without constant attention, your freelance pool can empty in no time at all.

Should you choose the in-house option, there are several routes that will take you to freelance talent.

Ex-employees

When hiring in-house, many organisations rely on ex-employees for freelance support. On the plus side, ex-employees will already be familiar with the way your culture and people operate. Equally, you will be familiar with their strengths and weaknesses. Existing staff are less likely to perceive ex-employees as a threat, which simplifies the assimilation process.

But this argument may work in reverse. An ex-employee may feel so comfortable in your organisation that he or she is ineffective at bringing about any change. At worst, familiarity can breed complacency as well as contempt. Rather than welcoming an ex-colleague's return, existing employees may resent the freelancer's new-found freedom – especially if it comes with more money, greater job satisfaction and easier access to your senior personnel.

So avoid the temptation to hire ex-employees just because they represent the line of least resistance. Instead, assess your needs objectively to ensure that the ex-employee is still the best person to fulfil them. If your objectives are relatively straightforward, an ex-employee may be perfect for the job. If you are trying to achieve something more radical, then a new broom may be a better bet. If change is your aim, relying on ex-employees might prevent your organisation from receiving a timely injection of fresh thinking and expertise. Furthermore, hiring an ex-employee could expose both of you to certain tax liabilities under IR 35 legislation (see Chapter 6).

Word of mouth and reputation

Word of mouth has always been a reliable route to freelance talent. Industry events, formal or informal networking and the trade press can help you keep up to date with the brightest freelance names in your sector. A freelance consultant's reputation can be a reliable indicator of quality, but it is often subjective and demands verification. Be clear about why someone is making a particular recommendation and establish what type of project the freelance consultant undertook on that employer's behalf. Word of mouth can turn into Chinese whispers, and people may tend to recommend freelance consultants they have heard of rather than actually worked with.

Always carry out your own research to ensure that behind the reputation stands a professional whose skills meet your specific needs. Some freelance consultants may have good reputations simply because they have a gift for promoting themselves. He who shouts loudest is not always your best choice. Furthermore, taking someone's reputation at face value could make you vulnerable to the 'star effect' – where enlarged reputations outweigh someone's ability to deliver, leaving you paying through the nose for an inferior service.

Allow your corporate brand to do the talking

Evaluate how effectively your organisation's brand is helping you find the freelance talent you need. Websites are becoming one of the most visible expressions of an organisation's brand values, yet their potential as recruitment tools is a long way from being fulfilled. Use your website to inform good freelance consultants that you are interested in their skills, and tell them how they can send you their details. If your brand profile is strong enough, you will invariably attract a high volume of unsolicited CVs from a broad cross-section of respondents. Better still, they come free of charge.

On the other hand, you may need to take a more proactive approach and advertise for freelance consultants in the most appropriate media. Advertising can be an expensive exercise so it is important to select the most suitable media. If you need to fill short-term assignments at short notice, online job boards and/or daily and weekly trade press titles are often the most effective option because they generate more immediate responses. When it comes to longer-term assignments, such as those involving maternity cover or an interim management position, the relatively relaxed timescales give you the luxury of using media with a longer shelf-life.

At times, it can pay to complement the role of your website as a brand promotion tool by taking out a broadly focused advertisement that also promotes your brand while emphasising the point that your organisation is freelance-friendly and always interested in receiving CVs from suitable people.

Having launched an advertising campaign, you must be prepared to manage the response. If you are a major brand or operate in a particularly popular sector or industry, prepare to be inundated. Even before an advert appears, decide who is going to handle the responses – line management or your HR team. Ideally, centralise the process and always ensure that those responsible for making it work have all the tools and resources they need.

As for responding to replies, you can always choose not to. But that is not a particularly wise move if you are hoping to promote your organisation as a client of choice among top-quality freelancers.

It is absolutely essential that you log every CV you receive onto some sort of database – preferably a searchable one. At the same time, bear in mind that freelance consultants – by their very nature – frequently switch assignments and direction, acquiring new skills and experience as they go. Consequently, their CVs tend to date quickly and keeping track of everyone's new skills and experiences is labour-intensive.

Tap into freelance networks

Instead of trying to source all your freelance requirements piecemeal and in isolation, consider tapping into the growing number of informal freelance networks. These networks comprise loose groups of individual freelance consultants who come together to share knowledge and new business opportunities. Some networks focus on offering one service. For example, there are networks of HR freelancers. Others offer a complementary cross-section of multi-disciplinary skills. Tapping into a freelance network could cut down on the leg-work, but you will still need to vet each person individually to ensure that he or she is suitable for your needs.

The rise of the online job market

Online recruitment – strengths and weaknesses

Strengths

- Reduced costs, increased speed
- Greater simplicity, enhanced control
- Compatibility with other e-business processes, notably e-HR
- Increasing Internet use.

Weaknesses

- Poor filtering
- Quantity of responses outweighs quality
- Limited market penetration
- Need for offline processes
- Too many low-quality sites.

In recent years, online recruitment has come of age as a strategically important recruitment tool serving all industry sectors at every level.

The dotcom boom was going to revolutionise so many aspects of modern life – especially the way organisations hire staff, both permanent and freelance. True enough, there was an explosion of recruitment websites and online job boards towards the end of the 1990s. When the dust settled after the boom went bust, it became clear that online recruitment is an excellent complement to conventional recruiting methods – but not necessarily a substitute. Indeed, current trends indicate that online and offline recruitment methods are quickly developing a symbiotic relationship.

More and more companies that manage their freelance resourcing in-house are using online job boards to post assignment briefs. This may involve using specialised industry portals or dedicated recruitment websites. Some of the more established names on an ever-changing list include totaljobs.com, monster.co.uk, workthing.com, fish4.co.uk. Other hiring organisations may prefer to post their assignment briefs on recruitment websites run by trade press titles or trade associations.

Key Note research forecasts that over the next five years, recruitment websites will focus on raising the quality of the people they provide by improving the way technology tests and filters them according to the relevance of their skills.

Researchers anticipate that if current trends continue, all major organisations will be using recruitment sites to advertise jobs and freelance assignments within the next two years. By then, around 10.3 million adults will be using recruitment sites to find job opportunities, compared to 6.2 million in 2002.

Online recruitment's principal strength lies in its ability to stimulate interest and solicit responses from a global audience – at little or no cost. But once the CVs have arrived, an organisation is still left with the labour-intensive and potentially expensive business of processing them.

In recent years, the most innovative recruitment websites have become increasingly effective at using technology to sift out suitable CVs. But in the interests of quality control, an organisation may still choose to outsource this process to an agency. Even then, however, freelance consultants with promising CVs still need to be vetted. And when it comes to vetting freelance consultants effectively there is no substitute for face-to-face contact with experts who know their own business as well as they know yours.

In the final analysis

It is now clear that hiring freelance consultants in-house demands a significant investment of time, energy and resources – even if you use online recruitment sites to handle some of the workload. To ensure that the required level of investment is forthcoming, commitment from the top of your organisation is essential. If no commitment is forthcoming, it is far simpler to contact a freelance resourcing agency.

OPTION 2: USING AN AGENCY TO HIRE FREELANCE CONSULTANTS

A guide to selecting the best agency

- To avoid costly misunderstandings, it pays to invest in establishing a sound relationship from the start. Does the agency understand exactly what you expect from it? Is it listening to your requirements – and are you communicating those requirements clearly?
- Does the agency appear genuinely enthusiastic about working with you to achieve your strategic goals?
- Is its freelance resourcing service core or peripheral?
- Is the agency forthcoming with the advice and guidance you need to make informed hiring decisions? For example, does it track changes in employment law and fluctuations in day rates?
- Does the agency understand the sectors you operate in? It is essential that the agency's staff have first-hand experience in your sector so they can read between the lines of a freelance consultant's CV.

- Does the agency have comprehensive vetting procedures? Unscrupulous agencies do not interview freelance consultants before submitting them. At the very least, make sure that any agency you use has interviewed all prospective freelance consultants, preferably face-to-face. Depending on the skill-set you are seeking, the agency may also need to conduct supplementary testing.
- How good is the agency at developing relationships with freelance consultants? Beyond sending you suitable CVs, the most effective agencies will work hard to build loyalty and trust among the freelance consultants on its roster. Initiatives such as networking events, newsletters, loyalty reward schemes and seminars keep freelance consultants up to speed with what you expect from them.
- Does the agency have robust back-office infrastructure? Simply tracking and approving time-sheets, for example, can be very time-consuming. To eliminate confusion and inefficiency, it is essential that the agency manages such administrative tasks rigorously – ideally online.
- Will the agency set up contracts on a legal basis that are sound enough to protect your position on issues such as copyright and confidentiality?
- Does the agency have transparent pricing to avoid any hidden surprises?

Although managing freelance talent in-house may appear cost-effective and straightforward, it can make disproportionate demands on your resources. What's more, the in-house option does not necessarily offer you any legal or commercial protection if an assignment goes wrong after you sign a contract with a freelance consultant directly. Agencies can offer a number of safeguards:

- *Consultancy*
  A good agency will work alongside you to define or refine your brief.

- *Choice*
  Using an agency invariably gives you access to a bigger pool of good-quality freelance consultants who have already been screened.

- *Speed*
  Credible agencies will have speedy processes for short-listing suitable and available freelancers.

- *Minimisation of contractual risk*
  Using an agency helps keep you in line with tax and employment law.

- *Minimisation of commercial risk*
  Ongoing contact between an agency and its freelance consultants helps to ensure that a project is completed to your satisfaction.

Clearly, agencies exist for very sound reasons – and the industry continues to expand. The UK has the largest recruitment market in Europe. According to the Recruitment and Employment Confederation (REC), the country's recruitment industry was worth

Table 4 / **Strengths and weaknesses of different agency types**

Type	Strengths	Weaknesses
Multi-sector; multi-nationals	Breadth Economies of scale Volume handlers	Non-specialist Sales-led, not service-led Impersonal
Large independents	Specialist knowledge Personal service Some scale	Lack breadth Can't handle large volumes
Small 'mom-and-pop' operations	Specialist knowledge Personal service Cheaper	Owner dependent Can't handle volume Poor systems/infrastructure
Online portals	Cheaper Can handle volume Fast Wide reach	Quantity, not quality No personal service Administration-heavy

£24.51 billion in the year to March 2004. Freelance/temporary/contract placements accounted for £22.81 billion of this total, while the permanent market was worth £1.7 billion.

More than half of Europe's freelance/temporary/contract placements are made in this country. Key Note forecasts that the UK's freelance/temporary/contract market will grow by 8 per cent by 2009 to £25.6 billion, while the permanent market will increase by 8.1 per cent to £1.87 billion over the same period.

The market offers an extensive choice of agencies and they vary widely in terms of quality, cost and approach. Their strengths and weaknesses are contrasted in Table 4.

Defining your needs

There is no right or wrong agency: the correct choice depends entirely on your requirements and your commercial reality – so be pragmatic. For example, if you need to fill a relatively high volume of non-specialist, temporary positions, then choosing a mainstream non-specialist agency is likely to be your wisest move. If you need to fill a more specialist position, logic dictates that you engage a niche agency.

The rates that niche agencies charge reflect the work they put into identifying, vetting, signing up and managing good-quality freelance consultants. In general, these agencies deal with accomplished professionals in the knowledge-based industries. Their talents are generally in high demand and their personalities have a significant impact on the organisations they work with. Finding someone with the right personality *and* skills for an assignment inevitably takes more effort than simply finding someone with the right skills. This translates into higher agency fees.

Investing in partnership

Making a partner out of your agency is not always obligatory or practical. At times it is not even desirable – especially if you have infrequent demands for freelance consultants and they are not important to your business model. But if you have regular requirements for professional freelance consultants who can add real value to your organisation, you are likely to derive greater value for money and expose yourself to less risk if you treat your agency as a partner rather than a supplier. The same principle applies to agencies, which should ideally treat freelance consultants as partners not commodities.

For many organisations, placing agencies on a preferred supplier list (PSL) is the first step towards partnership. But PSLs should not be treated purely as cost-cutting tools – especially in areas where personal chemistry and relationships are so important. Instead, PSLs should be used to protect service levels and maximise value for money. It is particularly important to emphasise this argument at a time when there is a growing trend towards involving purchasing and procurement teams in the recruitment process. Purchasing and procurement colleagues must understand that when it comes to hiring freelance consultants it is imperative that your agencies have the resources to provide you with the highest possible service levels. Saving a few pence here and there is inevitably a false economy and will almost certainly compromise any partnership you build with an agency.

That said, establishing a productive partnership with your chosen agency means investing time and resources up front. But if you want to ensure that you have reliable and regular access to the best talent, partnership is an investment worth making. It is essential to ensure that its foundations are sound from the start, so be clear about your needs.

If appropriate and possible, encourage your agency to develop an insider's knowledge of the way your organisation functions and where it is going. Getting under your organisation's skin helps an agency understand what sort of freelance consultant will support your long-term strategic objectives. To help this process, we suggest that you might:

- arrange for the agency to visit your offices
- introduce key agency staff to key people in your organisation
- give a presentation on your organisation's structure and activities. Include an overview of your HR strategy and your generic talent requirements for the next 12 months.

Bear in mind that partnership is a two-way street: the more you invest in getting to know your agency, the more you will get out of it.

Some large organisations with big requirements are appointing a single agency to manage *all* their freelance resourcing needs. Under these managed service contracts, the appointed agency even handles the relationship between its client and other agencies, which sub-contract into the umbrella agency. The main benefit of doing this when you have volume requirements is the potential cost-savings it can produce.

An agency specialising in placing freelance consultants can add value to your organisation by:

- investing time and resources into building a carefully profiled database of freelance consultants

- vetting CVs and interviewing potential freelancers

- building trust with freelance consultants

- keeping abreast of employment law

- keeping a watching brief.

Building a carefully profiled database of freelance consultants

Good freelance consultants don't simply walk through an agency's door. A creditable agency will spend time and money on targeting proven freelance consultants and convincing the best to register with it. It will invest in the freelance community through a number of channels – advertising and direct marketing campaigns, dedicated websites, loyalty reward schemes, networking events, and so on.

Unless your organisation is prepared to invest in-house resources into what is essentially a non-core activity, it is unlikely to match the breadth and depth of a database managed by an agency. Databases do not come cheaply, and the most professional agencies are prepared to invest in the latest technology to ensure that they can profile and access freelance talent efficiently.

Vetting CVs and interviewing potential freelancers

This is a notoriously labour-intensive step in the selection process. So labour-intensive, in fact, that the pressure it imposes is often reason enough to justify the cost of using an agency. The advantage of using a niche agency is that such agencies generally employ people with the first-hand sector knowledge required to read between the lines of every CV received. Soliciting good-quality CVs is difficult enough.

Equally challenging is the task of getting to know each freelance consultant individually, forming a detailed assessment of his or her strengths and weaknesses, aspirations and expectations. Ideally, an agency should use this information to build a personal and professional profile for all the people on its books. Having a bank of profiles on hand is helpful when there is an unexpected demand for freelance support. Indeed, an agency should devote the same effort to understanding its freelance consultants as it devotes to understanding your organisation.

> *Of course, we pay our agencies to carry out an initial vetting. But it's important to go further and find out exactly why someone really went freelance. Is it because they are really that good at what they do? Or are they just moving from assignment to assignment hoping not to get found out?'*
>
> Rachel Lucas, Lexis Public Relations

Less is more. An agency that is worth its fee will not inundate you with the names of potential interviewees. An agency that really understands your requirements will limit the number of CVs it sends you to between three and five. As its understanding of your business grows, this figure should decrease to below three. Of course, you can ask for as many CVs as you want. But if you are to truly benefit from using an agency, you must develop trust in its judgement, which will save you huge amounts of time.

Building trust with freelance consultants

Mutual trust is fundamental to the success of the three-way relationship between an agency, its clients and the freelance consultants that it places with them. According to the conventional laws of business, the client always comes first. But the best agencies give equal status to the freelance consultants on their books, working hard to build a strong sense of trust and community among them.

A good agency will not simply show interest in freelance consultants when considering them for a new assignment. Instead, it views the freelance consultants' next assignment in the context of their long-term career. In this sense, agencies perform the same role as an agent acting on behalf of an author, an actor or a professional sports person.

The rationale behind this fostering approach is straightforward: if freelance consultants do not feel that an agency is protecting their long-term interests, they are likely to take their expertise and experience elsewhere. Transparency between all three partners goes hand in hand with trust – especially when finances are involved. Inevitably, the trust-building process makes significant demands on an agency's resources. But without it, the client cannot expect to receive a high-quality service.

Understandably, such a high level of involvement is good news for freelance consultants. But how does it benefit you, the client? Again, it comes back to the horses-for-courses argument. Because credible agencies know their freelance consultants as closely as they know their clients, they can match both to produce a winning result. In certain cases, the depth of an agency's knowledge and the quality of its vetting procedures can eliminate the need for interviews because you are able to depend on its judgement. This helps to speed up the resourcing process significantly – another good reason to develop a close relationship with your agency.

Furthermore, many freelance consultants are either unable or reluctant to spend time on negotiating a fair fee. A significant number find the business of negotiating money embarrassing and are happy to trust it to their agency. Alternatively, they may not be up to date with current rates and may end up having unrealistic expectations or selling themselves short. Equally, many organisations prefer to focus on their core activities rather than keep abreast of changing market rates. By contrast, a proven agency stays up to date with prevailing day rates and can often predict how they will be impacted by changes in supply and demand. It will also maintain a transparent pricing system by splitting out its margins from the freelance consultant's day rate. Clearly, this benefits all three parties involved. (For a comprehensive overview of the financial aspects of using freelance consultants, see Chapter 6.)

Keeping abreast of employment law

This area is constantly changing and formidably complex – particularly when it applies to freelance consultants. Inevitably, keeping abreast of current legislation diverts precious resources from other parts of your organisation. An agency, on the other hand, will manage legal compliance as a core activity and deploy its resources accordingly. What's more, hiring freelance consultants through an agency should minimise your exposure to any legal risks.

Keeping a watching brief

You can choose to build your talent bank in-house or with the support of an agency. A growing number of agencies offer a watching brief service. This involves monitoring the freelance community on your behalf for an agreed period of, say, six months to a year. During this time, the agency will send you the details of any suitable people it finds.

Evaluating your agency relationship

Implement a six-monthly review process to assess your agency's service and the talent it has supplied. Standard metrics – or KPIs – that you can use to assess whether you are receiving a good service include:

- the number of CVs submitted compared with the number of interviews done
- conversion rates – the percentage of briefs that the agency has filled
- speed of conversion – the time taken to fill briefs
- the number of drop-offs: the number of placements that failed
- the average daily rates compared against budgeted rates
- the number of freelance consultants rebooked.

In addition, it is advisable to ask your in-house teams to give feedback on the quality of the freelance consultants the agency is supplying and on how closely they matched the brief.

CONCLUSION: AGENCY VERSUS IN-HOUSE

Using an agency offers strong advantages over identifying, hiring and managing freelance consultants in-house. Importantly, an agency will give you access to a greater breadth and depth of freelance talent. In addition, its vetting systems are likely to be tried and tested by experience.

Inevitably, cost is a factor and – as ever – you will generally get what you pay for. But the more an agency charges, the higher your expectations should be. In particular, expect the agency to develop an informed understanding of your organisation's culture and commercial realities.

On the other hand, you may not require particularly high levels of service and you might be perfectly happy for your agency to act as a supplier rather than a partner.

Ultimately, there are no hard and fast rules when it comes to using agencies, and it is important to be pragmatic.

Having decided whether to resource in-house or engage an agency, the next challenge is to ensure that you select the right freelance consultant to deliver your objectives.

Before the selection process

There are a number of issues to consider before beginning the selection process.

The importance of timely decisions

Before the selection process begins, be aware that the best freelance consultants are, by definition, invariably busy and will not necessarily wait for a slow decision from you. Naturally, they expect you to act quickly and inform them accordingly. Overall, the decision-making timeframe should reflect the length of the assignment as well as the urgency and importance of the project. Complex and strategically critical assignments demand a longer timeframe and will involve people higher up the management hierarchy. But freelance support is often required at short notice, and this means keeping the selection process as short as possible.

This principle works both ways: your organisation may require freelance support at short notice. So not only is it vital for your organisation to deal with freelance consultants in a timely fashion, it is equally important that the person you hire can master the brief at speed – a strength that always defines the best freelance consultants.

Personality counts

When hiring a suitable freelance consultant, his or her core skills will always be the most important factor in your decision. However, it is also important to consider what type of personality will best suit your needs and how a new personality will impact on your existing team dynamics.

For example, do circumstances demand a team player who fits into your organisation and its culture with minimum disruption, acting as a force for consolidation and continuity? Or are you looking for a devil's advocate capable of shaking things up with awkward questions that challenge the status quo? In reality, you are likely to require a combination of personal qualities.

Age versus experience

Legislation during 2006 is set to outlaw age discrimination in the job market, including the freelance sector. The new laws, combined with the intensifying skills shortage, are likely to force a change of attitude towards older freelance consultants. It is not uncommon, for example, to find that middle managers feel threatened by the very idea of hiring people who are older and more experienced than they are. But as skilled people become increasingly difficult to find, organisations may have no choice but to select older candidates.

Don't be distracted by job titles and seniority levels. Instead, focus on finding the key skills you require. Invariably, when buying freelance consultants you will be buying someone who is over-qualified for the task, which is what makes them so valuable to your organisation in the first place.

What's more, it is important to understand that freelance consultants themselves are generally disinterested in status and hierarchy. They are often more interested in job satisfaction and may even negotiate on their fee if an assignment interests them. By overlooking these factors, organisations are not only running the risk of breaking the law, they are also missing an opportunity to hire high-quality people very cost-effectively.

Ultimately, you should select the best person for the job.

When respect is due

The selection of permanent staff creates valuable opportunities to sell your organisation's strengths. The same applies to hiring freelancers. Take care to treat all the freelance consultants in your selection process with the same respect that you show to your permanent staff, clients and potential clients. Freelance communities can be tightly knit, and word of mouth spreads through them quickly. So if you fail to treat their members well, your organisation risks landing itself with a reputation as an organisation to avoid – a dangerous liability when talent is so scarce.

Beginning the selection process

Define your job description

This step is fundamental to the selection process. Split your criteria between desired or optional, and list the skills required. Because freelance consultants generally work to such tight deadlines, take care to avoid delays by prioritising your key requirements.

Brief your agency

When briefing your agency, be upbeat. They will only be able to sell it to their freelance consultants as positively as you do. Pay particular attention to:

- defining your needs
- setting a realistic budget
- setting a start date
- scheduling interviews
- sending interviewees a brief
- asking for references and examples of work
- defining the length of the contract
- establishing who pays the freelance consultant
- providing timely feedback on interviewees.

Interviewing

Aim to condense the interview process when hiring a freelance consultant, but stay alert to the commercial realities around you. Some roles will take longer to fill than others – especially those in which personal chemistry is a critical factor or for which the required skills are rare and/or in demand. Be pragmatic when weighing a freelance consultant's personality against your immediate requirements. It is not always necessary, for example, to complete psychometric tests or skill tests. Furthermore, there is no point in asking about a freelance consultant's long-term aspirations and career development needs. The important thing is to assess his or her track record. A freelance consultant is unlikely to stay with your organisation long-term. So focus on appointing someone who will get the job done rather than someone you hope might eventually retire as one of your board members.

Depending on the assignment, it is sometimes appropriate to send interviewees a brief before their interview. During the interview, ask them how they would meet the brief, paying particular attention to objectives and timings. Ensure that interviewees can support their suggestions by citing their past experience. Discuss in detail how they see your relationship developing during the assignment.

If relevant, ask interviewees to bring a portfolio of their work to the interview. This is common practice in creative sectors such as design, editorial, PR and advertising. Seeing a portfolio will enable you to evaluate someone's working style more accurately than reading a CV.

Sometimes interviews are not necessary. This applies particularly in the healthcare and IT sectors, where a freelance consultant's suitability for an assignment depends exclusively on professional skills. In these cases, most organisations are happy to be guided by an agency's recommendation.

If you do interview a freelance consultant, remember that he or she is also interviewing you. Choosing which clients to work for is often a major decision for freelance consultants, and their choice carries significant risk in terms of their reputation and income. Typically, a freelance consultant will draw conclusions about you, your organisation and the project based on answers to questions such as:

- Can I meet the brief? Can I add value or exceed the client's expectations?
- Do these people know what they want? Or are they going to change their minds constantly?
- Do I want to do it? Am I excited by this opportunity? Is it interesting? Will it add something to my profile?
- Do I like the organisation's people and culture? Can I work with them?
- Can they afford me? Will they be good payers?

Post-interview

Always ask for business references

These are particularly important when timescales are compressed and you expect to appoint a freelance consultant who can hit the ground sprinting – not just running. Indeed, there are some organisations that are prepared to eliminate the interview process to save time, relying instead on references and examples of past work. This option is best confined to skills-led roles.

Request a proposal

It is perfectly valid for you to ask an interviewee to submit a brief plan outlining how he or she would undertake the assignment, based on your discussions during the interview. At the same time, don't expect interviewees to spend time on an all-singing all-dancing proposal – unless you are prepared to pay for one.

Providing feedback

Providing timely feedback on interviewees gives you an opportunity to create goodwill between your organisation, your agency and the freelance consultants on its books. After all, you may need to hire more freelance support at short notice. Explain why you selected a particular person, but always let the agency know about unsuccessful interviewees. They might be suitable for future assignments and you don't want to burn any bridges.

Key point summary

- There are three ways to resource freelance consultants: you can do it in-house, by using online recruitment websites, or by appointing an agency.

- The in-house option demands a significant investment of time, energy and resources – even if you use online recruitment websites to handle some of the workload. It also demands buy-in at the highest level of your organisation.

- The principal strength of online recruitment is its ability to stimulate interest and solicit responses from a global audience – at little or no cost.

- But having harvested a bumper crop of CVs from unvetted respondents, an organisation is still left with the labour-intensive and potentially expensive business of processing them.

- Reputable and creditable agencies offer the benefits of expert guidance, speedy vetting and selection processes, a wider choice of freelance consultants, and protection from legal and commercial risks.

- The key to getting the best out of an agency lies in treating it as a business partner rather than as a supplier. Used correctly, agencies can add significant value to an organisation.

6

Understanding the legal framework

INTRODUCTION

One of the principal benefits of hiring freelance consultants is the legal and financial flexibility they give an organisation. Fortunately, the freelance tradition has a relatively long history in the UK. As a result, there is a robust set of proven measures in place that hiring organisations can use to protect their interests in any relationship with a freelance consultant. It is true that the EU has proposed moves to give non-permanent staff the same rights and entitlements as permanent employees. But at the time of writing, any decision appears to be some way off, and the freelance model still offers clients a high degree of control. For example, engaging a freelance consultant is still far more straightforward than taking on a full-time permanent employee. The same applies to letting one go.

When hiring freelance consultants, there are two things you must consider:

- Are you going to pay them a fixed price or according to time?

- Are you ever going to be their employer and, therefore, owe them employment rights?

At the same time, there are certain legal and financial issues that organisations should be aware of when hiring freelance consultants. In this chapter we give a brief oversight of the key areas that demand attention. Should you require more detailed advice, we recommend that you contact a recognised body such as the Chartered Institute of Personnel and Development (www.cipd.co.uk), the Recruitment and Employment Confederation (www.rec.uk.com, the association for the recruitment and staffing industry), or the Professional Contractors Group (www.pcg.org.uk, the representative body for the freelance small business community).

DEFINING A FREELANCE CONSULTANT'S EMPLOYMENT STATUS

Defining who is employed and who is self-employed

In certain circumstances, the employment status of your workers can have important financial and legal implications for your organisation. For example, if a freelance consultant does not fit the legal definition of a self-employed person, your organisation might become liable for tax and employers' National Insurance.

When determining a freelance consultant's employment status, you must consider three fundamental factors: personal service, mutuality of obligation, and control.

For *an employment relationship* to exist, all of the following must be true:

- There must be a requirement for 'personal service'. In other words, a named person is required to do the work, and the freelance consultant may not send a substitute to do some or all of the work.
- There must be 'mutuality of obligation'. This means that the freelance consultant is obliged to do work and the client is obliged to remunerate.
- The freelance consultant must work 'under the control' of the client.

All of these factors seem simple on the face of it. But all of them – in particular, the last two – are routinely the subject of lengthy and complex court cases. If these three factors are inconclusive for a particular engagement, other issues such as financial risk and the 'in business on own account' test for the freelance consultant may become determining factors.

It is worth pointing out that the tests which determine whether or not a freelance consultant is employed or self-employed for a given engagement (remember that status can and typically does vary from engagement to engagement) are precisely the same as those which determine whether or not the freelance consultant is subject to IR 35 (see page 91) for an engagement in cases where they operate through their own limited company.

Recent cases have militated against the historical assumption that the existence of a limited company removes the risk of the client being found to be the freelance consultant's employer. Clients who wish to protect themselves from this risk have to consider both the contractual terms and conditions under which they engage their freelance workers, and the actual working practices. The historical assumption that the interposition of a 'personal service company' removes this risk has come under question following some recent cases.

Before you engage freelance consultants, you must establish whether they will be regarded as self-employed or employed for your particular engagement, then ensure that their tax status reflects their employment status. Broadly speaking, a freelance consultant can work with you in three ways. Each has different implications for your organisation, as outlined in Table 5.

Table 5 | **The three ways in which freelance consultants work**

On PAYE	As a Sole Trader	In a Limited Company
Similar to permanent employment	Freelance consultant is self-employed	Freelance consultant is a company employee
Freelance consultant must submit P45 at beginning of each contract	Freelance consultant invoices you for fees and expenses	Limited company invoices you for fees and expenses
Freelance consultant cannot offset all expenses against the tax bill, only a limited subset	Freelance consultant is entitled to offset more reasonable set of expenses against the tax bill	Limited company is entitled to offset business expenses
You deduct income tax and NI at source	Freelance consultant pays income tax, Class 2 NI monthly by direct debit and Class 4 NI annually	Limited company deducts income tax and NI at source. Freelance consultant may receive dividend payments out of profits
Freelance consultant is entitled to statutory worker benefits and possibly full employment benefits	Freelance consultant is not entitled to statutory employment benefits	As a director/employee of the limited company, freelance consultant is entitled to statutory employment benefits, but they are provided and paid for by the limited company
Freelance consultant is entitled to paid holiday	Freelance consultant is not entitled to paid holiday unless later found to be a 'worker' under the Working Time Regulations	Freelance consultant is entitled to paid holiday, but it is paid by the limited company at no cost to the hirer
You undertake all administration	Freelance consultant must keep accurate records of all receipts and expenses for tax self-assessment	Limited company handles its tax affairs through corporate self-assessment and a company PAYE scheme. It must keep accurate business records of all receipts and expenses plus assets and liabilities
You are responsible for ensuring that the worker has the right to work in the UK and are required to have documented proof	You are responsible for ensuring that the worker has the right to work in the UK and are required to have documented proof	The limited company is responsible for ensuring that workers provided for it are legally entitled to work in the UK. It is responsible for ensuring that there is documented proof

Be aware that a freelance consultant's deemed employment status can vary from contract to contract. For example, freelance consultants may undertake work for one client and receive payment via PAYE while simultaneously working for another client as a sole trader or through a limited company.

It is important to emphasise that if you engage freelance consultants under a *contract of service*, and pay them using PAYE, they could be entitled to claim employees' rights such as holiday pay and sick pay, or even redundancy pay. Furthermore, you may be liable for unpaid employers' National Insurance and possibly income tax.

Recently, the courts (see *Cable and Wireless v Muscat* and *Hawley v Luminar Leisure PLC* and *Brook St v Dacas*) have suggested that this may be the case even if the freelance consultant works through a limited company.

None of these risks will apply if the worker is engaged under a *contract for services*, when a freelance consultant is paid gross. However, it is important to ensure that the contractual terms and conditions mirror your actual working relationship and the environment. This is because Her Majesty's Revenue and Customs (HMRC) and the courts take a dim view when contracts do not match reality. This applies particularly if the freelance consultant operates as a sole trader and you pay them gross.

It is difficult for a freelance resourcing agency to work with freelance consultants who operate as sole traders because the Inland Revenue stipulates (S134c ICTA 1988) that all agencies must deduct income tax and National Insurance at source when working with individuals. Sole traders, meanwhile, invariably want to be paid gross and sort out their own tax affairs. This consideration itself is the reason many freelance consultants work through limited companies. In some sectors, such as IT, this is almost exclusively the case.

One way that freelance consultants can get around this requirement is to register with an umbrella company. Not only do these companies handle time-sheets and invoicing on behalf of freelance consultants, they also take care of other time-consuming back-office tasks, arrange insurance and reduce the need for accountants – among other benefits.

As far as many freelance consultants are concerned, the biggest advantage of using an umbrella company is that it removes them from any involvement in the day-to-day running of a limited company. Effectively, umbrella companies give freelance consultants an alternative to working as a sole trader or through a limited company, even though it costs them. Significantly, if a freelance consultant uses an umbrella company, it rarely impacts on their clients.

Indeed, umbrella companies are safe as far as clients are concerned because there are numerous other freelance consultants working for the same organisation. However, it is not unheard of for organisations hiring freelance consultants via a third party to be found jointly liable for the freelance consultants' employment. To date this has only happened when the hiring takes place through an agency. There have also been a number of cases where HMRC has unwound arrangements relating to an umbrella or composite company arrangement. It is important to ensure that any umbrella company used by a freelance consultant you engage is set up correctly and pays the correct amount of tax, particularly in relation to the freelance consultant's expenses.

Umbrella companies are typically used by freelance consultants who think they will more or less always operate within IR 35. This is because the freelance worker will operate as a PAYE worker. The fees the worker pays to the umbrella company as well as PAYE taxes make it less cost-effective than the limited company. However, for work within IR 35 the difference is minimal and the umbrella company takes a lot of the administrative burden from the freelancer. More highly skilled and therefore more highly paid freelance consultants typically avoid umbrella companies in favour of their own limited companies.

If freelance consultants are not provided through an agency, extra care must be taken to ensure that nothing in the actuality of the engagement as well as in the contractual terms and conditions makes the hirer of the freelance consultant an employer. The risks – either of HMRC's investigating in pursuit of National Insurance contributions, or of a disgruntled freelance consultant's attempting to claim employment rights retroactively – should not be under-estimated.

Note that a written disclaimer signed by the freelancer stating that all parties wish the engagement to be regarded as self-employed has value against the former but is worthless against the latter, as the courts will regard it as possibly having been procured under coercion (even where, as in almost all cases, nothing could be further from the truth), and hence will disregard it.

As a rule, take particular care when engaging a freelance consultant who operates as a sole trader or through a partnership and receives payment gross. Operating via a limited company provides freelance consultants and the organisations that hire them with greater levels of security. The arrangement provides limited liability, enhanced insurance cover, clearer contractual obligations and stronger financial muscle. Indeed, many large PLCs will not deal with individual freelance consultants who operate as sole traders because it exposes them to unacceptable levels of risk through employment laws and other legislation. We would argue that the key to minimising your exposure when hiring freelance consultants lies in the contract you sign with them, as we explain in the following section. Note that it is important that the contract is more than a mere form of words. It must reflect the reality on the ground – otherwise, tribunals and other courts will disregard the contract and consider the real situation instead.

SETTING UP A CONTRACT FOR SERVICES

To ensure that a freelance consultant is not entitled to full employees' rights from your organisation, you should sign a contract for services with the freelance consultant's business. Do not sign a contract of service or an employment contract with the freelance consultant as an individual. It is, however, acceptable to ask the individual to sign confidentiality agreements on a personal basis because employment tribunals have found this not to affect employment status. Any contract between you and the freelance consultant must explicitly recognise the existence of the freelance consultant's company, with whom the contract is made. The freelance consultant should sign the contract in his or her capacity as the director of the service company.

At minimum, a contract for services should include the following clauses:

- a clause stating that there is no 'mutuality of obligation' between the parties. In other words, there is no obligation, on the one hand, for the freelance consultant to work, and on the other, for you to remunerate him or her. Where the contract is on a time-and-materials basis, this is often expressed as 'zero notice'. In other words, the freelance consultant may be dismissed immediately. Note that the freelance consultant may initially be reluctant to agree to this for commercial reasons, but there is a strong argument in terms of IR 35 risk for them to accept it. Alternatively, this may be expressed in terms that mean that where there is no work to be done, the freelance consultant will not be required to attend or do anything (and so will not be paid). This has the added advantage to the client that using the freelance consultant is restricted to when he or she is needed.

- a right of substitution clause allowing the work to be performed by another person provided by the freelance consultant's business. Usually, this should include terms covering areas such as right of veto, suitable qualifications, etc. A standard form of words that legal advisers have approved for this purpose is that the freelance consultant may supply a substitute subject to the client's acceptance that the proposed substitute has sufficient technical and professional skill to do the work, and that this acceptance will not be unreasonably withheld. It is helpful if logistical details (access to site, etc) are covered either within the contract or, more usually, in a separate letter given to the freelance consultant once the assignment begins. This is because should HMRC seek to challenge the arrangement as a sham to avoid tax, if practical details have been thought through and agreed, this is often enough to rebut the challenge. An advantage to the hirer of having a substitution clause is that should extenuating circumstances arise which prevent the consultant from continuing to provide the services, he or she would be responsible both for finding and for paying a substitute.

- a clause stating that the freelance consultant will not be subject to supervision, direction or control as to the manner in which he or she renders the agreed services. Freelance consultants are professionals who will use their own initiative when deciding how to deliver their services. This is often summarised in terms that state that the client decides 'what' and 'by when', and the freelance consultant decides 'how' and 'where' the work is to be done. It is helpful if the schedule of works under the contract is explicit rather than open-ended. For example, it could say 'This is a contract to produce a design for Project A', rather than 'This is a contact to provide design services for a period of time'.

- clauses covering copyright, confidentiality, payment, liability, IP rights and notice periods.

Any agreement or contract you sign should be worded to ensure that rewards are linked to the delivery of results rather than to job titles, tenure or status. Because freelance contracts are bespoke rather than off-the-shelf, the terms and conditions under which freelance consultants operate can vary widely. We have included some template contracts in the appendices (see pages 139, 151).

LEGISLATION TO BE AWARE OF

Areas of employment legislation that have a direct bearing on your relationship with freelance consultants include:

- IR 35 2000
- Working Time Regulations 1998
- statutory sick pay legislation
- Conduct of Employment Agencies and Employment Businesses Regulations 2003 (known as the Agency Regulations)
- the EU Agency Workers Directive (currently in its consultation stage)
- relevant immigration law in terms of the right to work in the UK.

Because there is so much controversy and uncertainty surrounding IR 35, we have provided a relatively detailed explanation of who it can affect and how. Otherwise, we have confined ourselves to brief summaries of the extensive legislation covering the hiring of freelance consultants and other non-permanent staff. Once again, to ensure that you are fully conversant with the most recent rules and regulations, it is advisable to contact a recognised body or an employment lawyer.

IR 35 – keeping a perspective

IR 35 can apply to anyone working through an intermediary, regardless of what they do. And the intermediary is normally a limited company, commonly referred to as a service company, although it could also be a partnership.

IR 35 was originally a numbered news release that appeared in the 1999 Budget. However, the concerns and controversy surrounding it have established it as a term in its own right. While many of the concerns may be legitimate, some of the controversy may be overblown. Although it is important to have an understanding of the regulations, we would argue that organisations should not regard them as a threat. They are primarily designed to give the Inland Revenue the flexibility required to collect employment taxes when the worker would not be classed as an employee. Flexibility is essential because – as we have emphasised already – freelance consultants work in so many different ways. Provided you follow the rules when engaging a freelance consultant, you will not be exposed. It is, however, important to have regard to recent cases in which freelancers have been found to be employees for all purposes and not just tax purposes, despite the existence of an intermediary limited company.

IR 35 – a brief history

The first part of the IR 35 legislation, affecting National Insurance only, was actually passed through Parliament at the end of 1999, although even this part did not kick in until the rest became law. The rest of the legislation, particularly those parts dealing with taxation, was enacted with the Finance Bill in the Spring 2000 Budget.

The Government's intention was, of course, to stamp out fraud and abuse of the tax system. Paymaster-general Dawn Primarolo claimed that there had been a recent increase in the number of people sidestepping the tax and National Insurance rules by setting up one-person limited companies. Ironically, the most usual reason for doing so was to allow the use of agencies, which are so commonly used in so many sectors.

At the time Ms Primarolo was quoted as saying: 'I have no sympathy for those who have been profiting unfairly from the present arrangements and whose complaint is simply that they don't want to pay their fair share of tax.'

Who does IR 35 affect?

Much of the publicity surrounding IR 35 has concentrated on its impact on the IT industry, in which a lot of contract work is carried out. But it would be wrong to assume that it applies only to people working in the IT sector.

IR 35 can apply to anyone who works through an intermediary, regardless of what he or she does. The intermediary is normally a limited company, commonly referred to as a service company, although it could also be a partnership.

The range of professions in which people work through such limited companies is wide. Examples include medical staff, chief executives of large corporates, legal and accountancy staff, construction industry workers, clerical workers, press officers, nightclub bouncers, and many others.

Basically, if a worker is claiming to be self-employed but is working under conditions in which he or she would be employed by the client were it not for the intermediate limited company or partnership, he or she is deemed to fall under IR 35.

What is IR 35 designed to achieve?

While it is often in the headlines, there is a degree of confusion over what IR 35 is actually designed to achieve.

Essentially, IR 35 legislation was introduced to counter what the Inland Revenue (IR) saw as 'disguised employment'. The classic example of this is the 'Friday to Monday' scenario, in which employees leave an employer on Friday and return as consultants on the following Monday. They do exactly the same work in exactly the same way, but work through their own limited company which pays them dividends, avoiding National Insurance.

Introducing IR 35 was designed to stop these one-person limited companies enjoying the tax benefits of self-employment while basically being full-time permanent employees.

Whatever the rights and wrongs of the measure – and arguments are vociferous on both sides – it is clear that IR 35 is a complex and subtle measure that has brought significant overhead to many legitimate freelancers.

The test for whether or not IR 35 applies sounds quite simple on the face of it. It is: if the freelancer were working directly for the hirer – ie if their own 'personal service company' and any agency were not there – would the relationship between freelance and hirer be one of 'employment' or 'self-employment'? In the former case IR 35 applies; in the latter, it does not.

However, the boundary between employment and self-employment is notoriously complex and many cases are heard in tribunals and higher courts each year. These higher courts have asked for more legislative clarity on the issue but to date successive administrations have not obliged.

Under IR 35, a further complication is introduced, in that one must consider a 'notional contract' that does not exist, and then apply the employment/self-employment tests to it. Where an agency is involved, this 'notional contract' may in fact be literally impossible to construct, because its nature will depend on clauses in the agreement between the agency and the hirer, which in the normal commercial course of events the freelance consultant has no business seeing. Notwithstanding, freelancers are expected to self-assess their liability to IR 35.

Although on the face of it IR 35 is the freelancer's problem and not the hirer's, it is difficult for anyone to argue that it makes sense for someone to be an employee for tax purposes but not for the purposes of employment rights. A number of recent UK tribunal cases have found freelancers to have been employed by their hirer (and thus owed termination rights, holiday pay, etc) despite the interposition of an intermediary limited company.

To protect against this, a contract for services as above should be used wherever it fits the reality of the engagement – and where it doesn't, consideration should be given to changing the nature of the agreement to protect against the cost of employment rights. This suits both the hirer, who will avoid liability for employment rights unwanted by either party to the deal, and the freelancer, who will be assured of working outside IR 35.

Further political moves within the EU are moving towards giving such 'workers' the same rights as employees. This is probably the motivation behind the EU Agency Workers Directive, since in the EU the freelance market is not nearly as mature as it is in the UK. Indeed, in some parts of the EU a 'worker' cannot use a limited company at all, and 'workers' are paid just like any other employee. Again, to protect against these moves it is important that contracts for services are used wherever such terms reflect the reality of the engagement.

What does IR 35 mean to your organisation?

To repeat: if you engage a freelance consultant who does not qualify as self-employed under IR 35 rules, your organisation may be liable for unpaid employers' National Insurance and income tax. According to the law, the freelance consultant is responsible for paying both. In practice, however, the Inland Revenue may ignore the contractual chain and seek to prove that the freelance consultant is *de facto* an employee in all but name, and tax him or her accordingly. In general, the Inland Revenue only seeks to recover unpaid National Insurance. The Inland Revenue may also look beyond the freelance consultant to include his or her clients. So to protect yourself, you must ensure that any contract matches the actual terms and conditions of the engagement.

Working Time Regulations 1998

If a worker is classified as an employee, he/she falls under the Working Time Regulations 1998. If a worker is not classified as an employee – in other words, if he/she is self-employed, working as a sole trader or through a limited company – the Working Time Regulations do not apply to him/her. However, as an organisation that might use freelance consultants and pay them through PAYE, you must be aware of the rules.

Paid annual leave

By definition, freelance consultants are not entitled to holiday pay unless they are also employees. All workers paid by PAYE are entitled to four weeks paid annual leave. This applies to freelance consultants who are paid through an organisation's payroll from the first day of employment or from the first day of working through a particular freelance resourcing agency. All workers are required to give notice before taking paid annual leave.

Paid annual leave is calculated as 8.33 per cent of a freelance consultant's day rate. If you are using an agency, you should check whether they are charging a rolled-up rate which includes the holiday pay or whether the agency is charging you statutory holiday pay as and when it is claimed by the freelance consultant. Either way, you need to budget for an extra 8.33 per cent on top of the day rate. In Scotland it is actually illegal to pay a rolled-up rate, but in the rest of the UK it is not. However, whoever is paying the holiday pay, the rules say that you must make sure that you split out the holiday pay separately on the freelance consultant's pay-slip and encourage him or her to take time off regularly.

Be aware that in cases where retrospective employment rights are being claimed, the monetary value in lieu of accrued statutory holiday pay can be very substantial. This is one reason why it is important to ensure that you use the correct contractual forms when engaging freelance consultants.

48-hour limit on the working week

On average, workers should not work for more than 48 hours in a week. However, they may agree in writing to work for longer. Freelance consultants can agree to work longer than the 48-hour week with the freelance resourcing agency by signing an opt-out provision.

The 48-hour limit is averaged out over 17 weeks (longer in some sectors), so there is some flexibility in the legislation. Nevertheless, you should make sure your freelance resourcing agency knows in advance if a freelance consultant is likely to work for more than 48 hours, particularly if he or she is new. In the first 17 weeks of the contract, the average working hours are calculated over the actual period that the freelance consultant has worked. For example, if a freelance consultant works 46 hours in Week 1 and 50 hours in Week 2 (making an average of 48 hours in the two weeks) and the assignment with you terminates, this will be within the law. But if a new freelance consultant works three 50-hour weeks in the first assignment with you, and that assignment then terminates, the regulations will have been breached – unless he or she has formally agreed to work more than 48 hours.

Rest breaks

All freelance consultants whose working day is longer than six hours are entitled to a rest break of 20 minutes. Ideally, they should be able to take this break away from their work station.

Night work

On average, freelance consultants should not work for more than eight hours in any period of 24. Night work is any three hours between the hours of 11 pm and 6 am.

Statutory sick pay

Only employees are entitled to statutory sick pay. So if you engage freelance consultants under a contract of service and/or pay them by PAYE, you will be liable. If you engage freelance consultants under a contract for services and pay them as a business, you will not be liable for statutory sick pay. Clearly, therefore, using the second type of contract provides more protection than the first. However, as with permanent employees, your company can reclaim approximately 92 per cent of what you pay out to freelance consultants from the Government.

Freelance consultants are entitled to claim sick pay as long as:

- they are actually engaged on the assignment for you when they become sick
- they are unable to work on normal work days for at least four days in a row, including weekends, as a result of sickness
- they can provide evidence of their sickness
- they are aged over 16 and under 65
- they are employed in the UK or an EC members state and are subject to the UK social security system
- they have not claimed any incapacity benefit, maternity allowance, invalidity pension or severe disablement allowance within the previous 57 days
- they have not been participating in a trade dispute either during or immediately before their sickness
- they are not within a statutory maternity pay period
- they are not in legal custody.

Conduct of Employment Agencies and Employment Businesses Regulations 2003 (known as the Agency Regulations)

This section explains how the Conduct of Employment Agencies and Employment Businesses Regulations 2003 (known as the Agency Regulations) affect you as a user of freelance resourcing services.

The Government introduced the Agency Regulations to raise standards within the recruitment industry. These regulations stipulate how a freelance resourcing agency should operate, providing added protection for freelance consultants and companies that use agencies.

Information an agency must supply you

According to the Agency Regulations, the agency must provide you with a contract setting out the agency's terms of business. The agency must also confirm the identity of the freelance consultant; that the freelance consultant has the experience, training and qualifications that you require for the assignment; and that the consultant is willing to undertake the project.

The agency must also obtain information about the position from you. This information should cover any health and safety risks you are aware of and the steps you have taken to prevent and/or control such risks.

Obligations to inform you if a freelance consultant is unsuitable

The Agency Regulations oblige agencies to notify you if they obtain information indicating that a freelance consultant may be unsuitable. This obligation applies throughout the assignment.

Restrictions on agencies' charging freelance-to-perm fees

Traditionally, agencies charge a fee if you take a freelance consultant on permanently directly after a freelance assignment. This is known as a temp-to-perm fee, or in our parlance a freelance-to-perm fee. Under the Agency Regulations, if you take a freelance consultant on directly, you may still be liable to pay a transfer fee – provided the agency gives you the option of an extended period of hire as an alternative to the fee. In addition the agency may only charge you a fee if you take on the freelance consultant within eight weeks after the end of an assignment, or 14 weeks from the start of the assignment (whichever is the later).

Freelance consultants who operate through their own limited company may opt out of the Agency Regulations if they so choose. This is beneficial to the agency but has little impact on the hiring organisation.

The regulations dealing with freelance-to-perm fees are complex. Once again, should you wish to obtain further information about them, we recommend that you contact a recognised body such as the Recruitment and Employment Confederation (www.rec.uk.com), the association for the recruitment and staffing industry.

Relevant immigration law affecting the right to work in the UK

Many freelance consultants work internationally, either as foreign nationals in the UK or as UK citizens working abroad. It is therefore important that you, or your agency, verify that any freelance consultant you hire is entitled to work in the UK. Failure to do so can result in a £5,000 fine for each individual under the Immigration and Asylum Act 1996.

Those who can work without a work permit or visa include:

- British citizens
- EEA nationals and Swiss nationals and their non-EEA family members exercising their free movement rights, and those nationals from the eight EAA accession countries who are required to register with the Home Office
- Commonwealth citizens with the right of abode in the UK

Those who can work without a work permit include:

- non-EEA overseas nationals with indefinite leave to enter or remain in the UK stamped in their passports
- those granted exceptional leave – for example, on compassionate grounds
- those with no restriction/prohibition on working stamped in their passports – for example, an overseas spouse of a British citizen or an EAA national, family dependants of a work permit holder
  (Note that some categories may require a visa to enter and work in the UK)
- Commonwealth citizens
  - who hold a working holiday-maker visa (subject to restrictions on type and length of work)
  - who have leave to remain derived from having a British-born grandparent
  - who are students undertaking a course of study for more than six months (subject to restrictions)
- others:
  - au pairs (limited to certain countries of origin and specific restrictions on type and length of work)
  - of miscellaneous categories – for example, seasonal agricultural workers or employees of overseas companies on secondment.

Secondary legislation came into force on 1 May 2004. In the case of incorporated workers it is their limited company which becomes legally responsible for ensuring that they are entitled to work in the UK, and if they choose to opt in under the Agency Regulations (or rather, don't opt out), the agency *must* also check their ID. There is a risk, however, where someone is found 'effectively to be the employee of the hirer' that the responsibility to check the right to work in the UK – which rests with his or her limited company – transfers to the hirer like all the other responsibilities of an employer.

EU Agency Workers Directive – legislation under development

The European Commission introduced this directive in March 2002. It aims to give temporary workers the same pay and conditions as permanent staff. In the UK there is significant resistance to the Directive in its present form. If introduced, there are concerns that the ruling would make the UK labour market less flexible when it comes to employing non-permanent staff, including freelance consultants. Some organisations representing UK companies are counter-lobbying for greater flexibility in European labour markets.

The REC's position is that the derogation period on pay and conditions must be as long as possible, and certainly longer that the six weeks mentioned in the current draft. The REC is seeking a year's derogation to be consistent with other qualifying employment rights.

The REC is also seeking an 'adequate level of pay' for agency workers, which would be defined as:

- at least a minimum of the pay scale, where one exists, and
- at least the national minimum wage where there is no company pay scale.

HEALTH, SAFETY AND WELFARE: YOUR RESPONSIBILITIES TO FREELANCE CONSULTANTS

Your organisation is legally responsible for protecting the health, safety and welfare of all its employees and sub-contractors while they are working on your premises or using equipment or substances that you provide. This ruling applies to self-employed freelance consultants and other non-permanent staff – even if they are supplied by an agency.

When briefing an agency or interviewing prospective freelance consultants, inform them of any specific risks or hazards highlighted by your standard risk assessments. Also inform them of your rules on smoking, and any requirement for long working hours. Provide them with copies of your written health and policy statements.

Your introduction procedures should cover health and safety issues. As a legal minimum, freelance consultants are entitled to be shown fire exits and assembly points, first aid provision, accident recording arrangements, and your smoking rules.

Where appropriate, freelance consultants are also legally entitled to well-designed and ergonomically sound workstations. Although you are not obliged to provide eye tests for freelance consultants working with computer screens, they should be encouraged to take regular breaks of five minutes every hour.

What insurance cover should freelance consultants have?

There are a number of mandatory and optional insurances for freelance consultants.

Personal insurance

Freelance consultants who work from home must ensure that their home office and any work equipment is either covered by their home contents insurance or business-specific insurance. Laptops are usually not covered by home insurance. If they use their own car when travelling on business, they must take out appropriate motor insurance. The minimum requirement is Class 1 Business Use insurance.

Professional indemnity insurance

Professional indemnity covers professionals against litigious claims for negligence. It applies to errors in advice as well as service provision, and covers legal liabilities and the mitigation of consequential loss.

It is important to establish whether your freelance consultants have professional indemnity insurance, especially if they would face particularly serious risks if an assignment with your organisation goes wrong. After all, few organisations would choose to deal with the conflict and cost of settling a disputed claim with an individual.

Litigation against freelance consultants, particularly in the IT sector, is on the increase. This trend is very visible in the USA and is heading towards the UK. A growing number of organisations, especially the public sector, are demanding that freelance consultants have professional indemnity insurance. The most professional freelance consultants recognise their responsibilities to minimise their clients' concerns. Those without the appropriate cover will find it increasingly difficult to win business at a time when organisations are placing increasing emphasis on identifying and managing all risks associated with their activities.

Gary Head is UK Underwriting Manager, Hiscox Insurance Company Ltd. He describes professional indemnity insurance as a 'sleep-easy' that helps to ensure that freelance consultants are not distracted from their core work. 'Unlike professionals working for large organisations,' he points out, 'freelance consultants have everything to lose if things do go wrong, including their house and their reputation. They also face the risk of bankruptcy. At the very least, a freelance consultant's personal indemnity insurance pays for their legal defence – provided they have acted within the law.'

Employers' liability insurance

This is a legal requirement for all limited companies except for one-man bands. It insures employees against injuries caused in the workplace. By law, cover must be for at least £5 million. As soon as freelance consultants operating as one-man bands have someone else working in their office – whether as sub-contractors or employees – then they are obliged to have employers' liability insurance in place.

Public liability insurance

This covers any damage a freelance consultant might cause to the public in the course of work. It applies to freelance consultants who operate as a limited company. You need to decide whether to insist that they have this insurance depending on the nature of the work that they are undertaking for you.

Permanent health insurance

Because freelance consultants are not entitled to statutory sick pay from clients, permanent health insurance acts as a vital safety net for them. Their private arrangements do not affect your organisation.

Pensions

Your organisation has no responsibility for a freelance consultant's pension arrangements. Because freelance consultants do not have the benefit of a company pension scheme, they are responsible for their own retirement provision. Some agencies operate their own stakeholder pension schemes for the freelance consultants on their books, although they rarely make contributions to them.

Key point summary

- The UK has a robust set of proven measures that hiring organisations can use to protect their interests in any relationship with a freelance consultant.

- Nevertheless, a freelance consultant's employment status can have important legal and financial implications for your organisation.

- Before engaging a freelance consultant, establish whether he or she will be defined as self-employed or employed for your particular engagement.

- For a 'self-employment' relationship to exist, there must be no 'personal service', 'mutuality of obligation' or 'control' by the client.

- Minimise any possible exposure by ensuring that your freelance consultant's tax status reflects his or her employment status.

- To ensure that a freelance consultant is not entitled to full employees' rights from your organisation, sign a *contract for services* with the freelance consultant's business and not a *contract of service*. See Appendices.

- Make sure that the contract is more than a mere form of words and reflects the reality on the ground.

- When hiring freelance consultants, there are five key areas of employment legislation to be aware of, alongside relevant immigration laws: IR 35 (2000), Working Time Regulations (1998), statutory sick pay legislation, Conduct of Employment Agencies and Employment Businesses Regulations (2003) and the EU Agency Workers Directive (currently in consultation).

- IR 35 was designed to stop one-person limited companies enjoying the tax benefits of self-employment while basically being full-time permanent employees.

- Some of the legislation is controversial, but provided you follow the guidelines explained in this chapter, it should cause no serious problem to your organisation.

7

Getting the best from freelance consultants

We seem to have struck a sound balance between the permanent model and the freelance model. Associates value the freedom of freelancing but also identify strongly with Ashridge and what it stands for. The next challenge is to continue to develop the way we manage them.

Fiona Dent, Director of Executive Education, Ashridge Management College

INTRODUCTION

There is a clear consensus that freelance consultants can be an expensive luxury if they aren't managed effectively. But one of the most common concerns we encountered while researching this book is the scarcity of formal and tested guidelines on managing the freelance model. It is a concern shared by organisations in all sectors as well as HR professionals and the academic community.

A 2002 report jointly published by the Economic and Social Research Council and the Open University Business School pulled no punches when addressing this issue. *The Price of Freedom: The myths and realities of the portfolio career for experienced older professionals* notes that the position of freelance consultants in its study was undermined by a lack of strategic management practices.

> *In terms of the day-to-day management of freelancers, there seemed to be a lack of formal policies, codes of good practice or systematic management tools within organisations. Coupled with the absence of widely-accepted and enforceable industry standards, this led to highly variable practices.*

According to the report, these practices included unfair recruitment decisions, poorly specified briefs, inaccurate estimates of the amount of work involved, inadequate compensation for work completed and insufficient feedback at the end of an assignment. What's more, the report identified an overall lack of transparent systems for locating and retaining freelancers and for making employers accountable to their freelance professionals.

The author and academic Charles Handy has said:

> *Many organisations really do not understand how to manage freelance consultants because they are no good at allowing creativity to happen. . . . Organisations that are able to live with*

this tension will grow rapidly. They understand that fleas are often highly accomplished at delivering, but they like to be left alone. They don't want to answer to a boss or to comply with bureaucracy. In essence, they are professionals who don't want to be made into employees because it makes them feel trapped.

So how does an organisation avoid the elephant traps? According to Richard Baines, Director of the London-based human resources consultancy Argyll HR:

The answer lies in managing freelance consultants with the same rigorous professionalism that you apply to permanent staff. This may seem obvious, but in the UK it is only just starting to happen. This lack of rigour is symptomatic of common attitudes towards using freelance consultants.

The Work Foundation's deputy director of research, David Coats, argues that failure to manage the freelance model adequately could offset whatever value it can add to an organisation. 'Management must address three key questions,' he notes.

First, how do you control the entry of freelance consultants into your organisation? Second, how do you integrate them with your existing staff once they have arrived? Finally, how do you manage their exit from your organisation? In other words, what information and knowledge are they taking with them, and how much of your institutional memory do you lose when they go?

As far as David Coats is concerned, the debate is not about whether the future is in the hands of freelance or permanent workers. Instead, the fundamental question is: how does an organisation negotiate and embed change? 'Whether you achieve that with permanent staff or freelance consultants is neither here nor there,' he advises.

PART 1: SETTING THE FRAMEWORK

Pre-assignment checklist

Before a freelance consultant begins work, ensure that you have both reached agreement on the following points. Not every point will be relevant to every assignment, so tailor the checklist accordingly. If necessary, agree each point in a formal, signed contract – but be aware that signing a contract does not guarantee the outcome you require. From the start, it is essential to invest time in building the trust that underpins successful freelance relationships.

- objectives
- deliverables
- timescale/milestones
- start date
- trial period
- terminating early
- costs (fees, expenses, taxes, agency fees)
- invoicing/payment procedures

- timesheets/logging (if applicable)
- working place/modus operandi
- culture
- additional resources
- reporting lines, approval processes, authority levels
- confidentiality/client contact/intellectual property
- IT/health and safety/environmental/ethical policies
- evaluation
- knowledge transfer
- exit.

Through consultation with a representative cross-section of organisations and agencies, research bodies and academics, we have drawn up a set of guidelines on how to get the best from freelance consultants, whose contributions to the consultation process were also vital. Getting the best out of freelance consultants is far from an exact science. It has often depended on the subjective assessment and gut instincts of those responsible for hiring them. Our guidelines are designed to be as pragmatic and flexible as possible. Adapt them to your particular requirements, taking account of your organisation's size, risk levels, budgets and timescales. Wherever possible and appropriate, incorporate the guidelines into any contract you sign with a freelance consultant.

In general, you need to manage freelance assignments just as you manage other business processes. When hiring a freelance consultant, it is important to be clear that you are seeking to establish a business-to-business relationship with him or her rather than an employment relationship. As with any other business-to-business relationship, the key to a productive partnership is in the briefing.

But before signing anything, a word of caution from Handy:

> *Don't rely on a contract that is simply based on a set of guidelines because it takes no account of the psychological contract between you and the freelance consultant. And when it comes to creating a loophole-free psychological contract with freelancers, nothing counts more than trust. That's why it is so important to invest time in building a mutually productive partnership with them. This demands commitment up front, but ultimately it will enable you to build a strong element of reliability into the delivery of your products and services. And in the long run, reliability saves priceless time.*

Fiona Dent of Ashridge Management College agrees. 'Ultimately,' she notes, 'our relationship with our associates is based on trust. In fact, we don't even ask them to sign formal contracts. Instead, we have an associates' charter outlining what we expect from them – and what they can expect from us.'

When recruiting to fill a permanent position, discussions between employer and applicant tend to be relatively vague. Generally, this is because permanent jobs are regarded as long-term and the focus is therefore on aspirations, personal growth, future challenges.

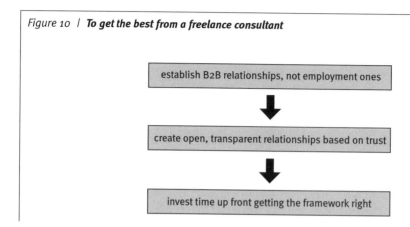

*Figure 10 | **To get the best from a freelance consultant***

Developing a productive relationship with a permanent employee generally begins once the interview process is over and once he or she is settled in the new position. Although employees begin work with a written job description, their personal and professional development usually evolves as they grow into their role.

By contrast, you will not necessarily enjoy the luxury of time when hiring a freelance consultant, whose assignments – by their very nature – are temporary. Setting up a transparent, mutually satisfactory agreement with a freelance consultant demands detailed discussion and greater clarity – *before* the assignment begins. A freelance consultant should not start work without a clear set of objectives and key performance indicators (KPIs) at the very least.

When drawn up correctly, an agreement with a freelance consultant becomes a case study in honesty and partnership. Before signing, both parties are free to discuss any issues and concerns while establishing their expectations and requirements. Although the perfect agreement may take time to set up, once it is in place it should manage itself.

In Chapter 1 we examined the results of research conducted by Leeds Metropolitan University in partnership with freelance resourcing agency Xchangeteam. Among other findings, this research reveals that hiring organisations place particular value on a freelance consultant's ability to 'hit the ground running' and regard those who have that ability as 'easy to manage'. But just because a freelance consultant is easy to manage does not mean that hiring organisations can simply take him or her for granted. On the contrary, it is essential to invest in a robust management framework for freelance consultants – otherwise, they will find themselves working in a vacuum where they are unlikely to perform to their full potential. But once the management framework is set, freelance consultants are, indeed, generally less time-consuming and more straightforward to manage. Goal-oriented and programmed to get the job done, they are less likely to become distracted from the objectives they have agreed with you. They are, for example, generally reluctant to become involved in office politics.

Another note of caution: when building relationships with freelance consultants, don't neglect your existing staff. Honest communication is imperative whenever the issue of freelance consultants arises. Reassure your staff that bringing in external support is not a sign that they have failed. Rather, it demonstrates decisive management: your organisation has identified a priority and selected the most effective means of addressing it. Wherever possible and appropriate, explain the freelance consultants' role, what they are expected to achieve, and how they will interact with the organisation. In other words, the level of authority they hold and their reporting lines. In addition, explain why their support is necessary. Presenting your case positively and openly will encourage staff buy-in. If people feel that they will be able to learn from a freelance consultant, they will be even more inclined to welcome him or her. One essential point: introduce freelance consultants to the people they will be working with *as soon as possible*.

AGREE YOUR OBJECTIVES

It is worth repeating that the key to maximising the value of a freelance consultant lies in agreeing a set of clearly defined objectives with him or her. Ideally, these objectives should be signed off before the assignment starts and monitored on a regular basis throughout.

Because freelance assignments vary so widely in nature and scope, it is not possible to produce a generic template for drawing up objectives. Some assignments demand intangible outcomes; others call for easily demonstrable and measurable outcomes. For example, an ailing organisation may hire an interim CEO to restore its fortunes. Another organisation may appoint a freelance internal communications consultant to foster a more productive working relationship between two divisions. Clearly, the objectives you agree for these two projects will be more complex than those you agree for a relatively straightforward, self-contained assignment involving, say, a customer survey.

As a rule of thumb, the more intangible the desired outcomes, the more precisely your objectives need to be spelled out. Tangible or not, you must be clear about what you hope to achieve before you can agree an effective brief or establish a set of KPIs to measure your progress. The answers to the following questions will help to ensure that any objectives you set are relevant and achievable:

- Does the project have specific outcomes?
- Do you need to complete the project by a certain time?
- Does the project require people management?
- Does the project involve the delivery of a product or intellectual property?
- Does the project involve implementing change?
- Does the project involve the delivery of strategy and advice?

Provided you set your objectives according to the SMART principles and agree them up front with the freelance consultant, it should be possible to measure them. Under SMART principles, objectives should be:

- **S**pecific – involving an observable action or achievement linked to a rate, number, percentage or frequency

- **M**easurable – incorporating a mechanism to track and record the specifics defined above

- **A**chievable – possible to complete with a reasonable amount of effort and application

- **R**elevant – with a meaningful impact on the organisation

- **T**imed – with the start and/or finish dates clearly defined.

It is quite possible that you have a limited understanding of the skills a freelance consultant is bringing to your organisation. If you already had his or her know-how, why would you have to import it? If your lack of understanding concerns you, research current industry benchmarks and standards. Among other benefits, this will place you in a better position to judge what levels of service your freelance consultant should be providing once he or she starts work. Trade and industry bodies are a useful source of this information. Other useful sources include your freelance resourcing agency and any other freelance consultants that you have a relationship with. If they fail to produce the information you require, we suggest that you use the first week of the assignment to clarify your objectives in collaboration with the freelance consultant. This is where a freelance consultant's diverse experience on how to approach different projects is particularly useful.

DEFINE DELIVERABLES

From the outset, foster open debate about what your freelance consultant must deliver to meet your agreed objectives. Deliverables vary from sector to sector, assignment to assignment. They might include a piece of research, a signed-off specification, a set of process maps, a press release, a software programme, or proposals for an advertising campaign. When managing large, complex and technical projects, you may need to drill a long way down into the specific activities before you are able to define exactly what the freelance consultant should be delivering. But provided a deliverable is tangible and tailored to the assignment, you should be able to chart its development against your agreed objectives.

Like objectives, however, some deliverables are more tangible than others. Corporate change programmes are a notable example of projects with deliverables that are difficult to define – and tricky to measure. Their true impact can take years to reveal itself. Challenges also arise when a freelance consultant is selling his or her intellectual property rather than his or her time. After all, a deliverable that is unique to a particular person is always difficult to compare and, therefore, measure. In this case, it is important to research the freelance consultant's style and track record in detail *before* deciding whether he or she is the right person for your organisation. You should monitor progress against your research conclusions.

When agreeing the deliverables, draw on the experience of your freelance consultants. They are likely to have been involved in agreeing a wide variety of briefs, and it is precisely this knowledge that you are paying for. In the final analysis, clear and agreed deliverables are essential to ensuring that freelance consultants deliver positive results – and value for money.

SET TIMESCALES AND MILESTONES

When agreeing schedules, be realistic – then add a contingency. Incorporate review points throughout the duration of the assignment. Whether reviews take place by phone or email, in writing or face-to-face, it is vital to keeping a project on track by answering critical questions such as: is the project going into too much depth, or not enough? Is it meeting its objectives? Do we need to modify the deliverables? Will it lead to the desired outcomes? Milestones set before an assignment starts will provide invaluable points of reference once work has commenced. But as work progresses, be prepared to modify the milestones.

Changing circumstances may mean that you might have to extend or compress timescales, two options that could impact on costs. If timings extend, you may have to provide the freelance consultant with additional support and resources. If timings compress, you may have to pay a premium to meet the deadline. He or she may be pre-booked for another assignment, so flag up any schedule changes as early as possible to avoid any availability problems. Take care never to blame a freelance consultant if timings slip due to circumstances beyond his or her control.

SET A START DATE

Set a realistic start date. The scarcer the expertise ands skills you require, the longer it will take to find a freelance consultant to deliver them. This makes forward planning essential. Furthermore, the best freelance consultants are generally in demand long-term, so book them as far ahead as possible. Give your organisation plenty of time to prepare for the freelance consultant's arrival. The better your preparation, the more benefit you will derive from the freelance consultant because he or she will be able to hit the ground running. Once the freelancer is on board, allow enough time to give him or her a thorough briefing. Before starting work, it is possible that the freelance consultant may raise valid issues. Ensure that you build in enough time to address them.

SET A TRIAL PERIOD

Setting a trial period can be important if you have not used the freelance consultant before. Trial periods are frequently used to judge whether the personal chemistry is right. But they are not always necessary – or possible. For example, you might hire a freelance consultant specifically because you require quick results in specific areas.

If your timescales are tight, if personal chemistry is not an issue, then trial periods are hardly necessary. Then again, trial periods need not be lengthy and should always be set according to the complexity and length of the project. Once you have agreed a trial period, be clear about who decides whether it has been satisfactory – and what criteria are to apply. Transparency is essential to ensuring that freelance consultants do not become scapegoats for management or organisational failure.

TERMINATING A FREELANCE CONTRACT EARLY

Not all freelance assignments work out. Responsibility for any failure could lie with the freelance consultant, with your organisation – or in a combination of factors. Typical reasons for terminating a contract include:

Freelance consultant:

- personality clashes with existing employees
- poor understanding of your internal culture
- too experienced or inexperienced
- poor-quality work
- high costs.

The hiring organisation:

- office politics
- poor planning and management
- change in budget
- switch in direction
- insufficient resources to achieve goals.

You should analyse any demands to get rid of a freelance consultant before you take a decision. Bear in mind the reasons you hired freelance support in the first place. You might find, for example, that the permanent staff are resistant to changes that the freelance consultant was briefed to implement.

If a freelance consultant is proving unsatisfactory, your options will depend on the scale and scope of the project, its complexity and whether the freelance consultant is responsible for a specific deliverable or is working as part of a project team. Your organisation's first instinct may be to get rid of an under-performing freelance consultant immediately. But if his or her knowledge is indispensable or if the project has reached a critical point, it is often wiser to line up a suitable replacement before terminating the contract.

One of the major benefits of using freelance consultants is that terminating your relationship with them can be relatively painless. However, many freelance contracts incorporate a notice period that should be respected, unless the freelance consultant's behaviour demands instant dismissal. This would usually apply, for example, in the case of gross negligence.

So you have two choices:

- Flag up your concerns with the freelance consultant; discuss them constructively, preferably face-to-face; agree possible solutions; and set a review date.

- Explain why you are serving him or her with notice immediately, taking into account any notice period you have agreed, unless there has been gross negligence.

In practice, many organisations deal with these situations by simply allowing their contract with the freelance consultant to come to an end and never using him or her again. This is an unsatisfactory solution for both parties, particularly because it prevents any discussion about why the relationship did not work. Such discussion can be illuminating and often surprising. What's more, it often provides invaluable lessons on how to modify management processes and use freelance consultants more effectively in future.

NEGOTIATE COSTS

Freelance fees

Time and materials

The majority of freelance consultants use time as the basis for determining their fees. Time has become the basis for setting fees because it can flex according to variations in the scope and/or delivery of a project, and therefore mitigates any risk the freelance consultant might face. In this respect, they are no different from professional service companies such as management consultancies, marketing agencies or legal practices. Freelance consultants who sell their time are generally paid a weekly rate, a day rate or sometimes an hourly rate. The most common of these is the day rate. When agreeing a day rate, prepare to be led by the market. The market works on the assumption that freelance consultants will only be able to charge for a certain proportion of working days during the year. This proportion varies between three-quarters and two-thirds. Whatever the exact figure, a freelance consultant's day rate needs to compensate for scheduled downtime, which might add up to as much as three months out of every 12. Unfortunately, the fact that the most successful freelance consultants often work at full capacity throughout the year does not necessarily mean that they will agree a lower day rate with you. On the contrary, they might even cite the laws of supply and demand in their defence before demanding a higher day rate! When agreeing a day rate, it is often worthwhile ensuring that everyone understands what is meant by a professional working day. Usually there is no issue, but it is better for any disagreements to surface while agreeing terms than once an assignment has started.

Assignment fees or fixed fees

Rather than charging by time, some freelance consultants choose to charge a fixed price to complete a specific service or product. But generally, charging a fixed price is only a viable option for freelance consultants if they have significant control over the scope of the project and the process involved. Without this control, they run the risk of undercharging their client and short-changing themselves because in practice the brief often changes as the business environment shifts, sometimes radically and in mid-project. This is why in many sectors, time and materials agreements often dominate.

Clearly, the scarcer the skills required to deliver a specific product or service, the more expensive they become. Increasingly, freelance consultants will seek to work on an assignment fee basis, because it almost always protects them from IR 35 liability.

Overtime

By definition, overtime payments apply to freelance consultants working on a time and materials basis only. Once again, it is important to reach an agreement before the assignment starts and include it in your contract. Note that day rates usually include reasonable overtime worked during the normal working week, but for hourly paid freelance consultants, you will need to agree the number of hours in a working day, whether the freelance consultant charges overtime by the hour or as a proportion of the working day, and whether the day rate or hourly rate increases on weekends and public holidays.

Expenses

Before the assignment begins, agree with your freelance consultant what expenses you will pay him or her, and how often. Typically, sole traders and freelance consultants operating through a limited company attach any expenses to their regular monthly invoices. Freelance consultants working on a PAYE basis will need to submit expense claims using your in-house expenses system. Whatever agreement you reach should be included in the contract you sign.

Success bonuses

Success bonuses are relatively rare, but they can act as a useful negotiating tool. Judiciously employed, they can help to bridge the gap between your budget and the freelance consultant's expectations. The added benefit of success bonuses is that they are a very effective way of securing a freelance consultant's commitment to getting the job done while optimising the quality of his or her work.

The fees that freelance consultants charge vary widely according to their reputation, level of experience and the sector or industry that they operate in. Supply and demand in the freelance market also affects their earning power: when skills are in short supply and high demand, fees rise – and fall when skills proliferate and demand falls.

It is important not to fall into the trap of comparing day rates with an annual salary: you will not be comparing like with like. As we explained in Chapter 2, there are many hidden costs associated with employing people on a full-time permanent basis. These costs – which might include benefits, training and support staff – must be factored into the calculation. Too often, however, they are forgotten. If you look at the *total costs* of employing a permanent person on a daily basis against a freelance consultant's daily rate, then you will be comparing like with like.

Counting the hidden costs on your payroll

Nick Robeson is chairman of the UK-based Interim Management Association. In his experience, a freelance consultant's day rate generally equates to 1 per cent of the annual salary he or she would earn as a full-time permanent employee. At the senior end of the scale, interim managers work an average of 180 days compared to 242 days worked by full-time permanent workers. But while freelance day rates may appear high, remember that they do not include the hidden costs associated with full-time permanent employees. These can inflate monthly pay cheques by 50 per cent or more. Hiring freelance consultants can mean paying a premium of between 25 and 30 per cent for experience and flexibility – plus the talent to deliver results within short timescales.

In Chapter 6 we explained how a freelance consultant's employment status is likely to influence the rate he or she proposes. In other words, the daily rate of self-employed consultants can be higher because it will take into account all other 'working costs' such as pension and benefits, and the client will not be responsible for associated taxes. Those being paid by 'payroll' will attract extra costs such as National Insurance and some statutory benefits. Their rate is therefore likely to be lower.

Invariably, you will get the quality of freelance consultant you pay for. Before opening negotiations, establish whether you need the Deluxe GT or bog-standard Runner option. Begin by asking the freelance consultant what rate he or she charges. Freelancers will often quote a price range. As negotiations progress, be guided by the market and by your freelance resourcing agency – if you are using one. Some sectors and industries have fixed fee rates for certain types of freelance work. In such cases, negotiation is unnecessary. Bear in mind that the best freelance consultants are invariably in high demand. As a result, they are not always open to negotiation anyway. If you haggle unnecessarily, they will simply take their expertise elsewhere.

What is a typical day rate?

Day rates vary enormously between sectors and industries and of course, levels of experience. Tables 6a–f present a few examples of what you could expect to pay freelance consultants in different circumstances.

Table 6a–f | ***Freelance rates guides***

Communications and PR freelance rates guide	
Freelance level	**Daily fee band**
Account executive or an equivalent	£100–150
Senior account executive / Account manager or equivalent	£120–200
Account director / Associate director or equivalent	£200–350
Director or specialist senior consultant	£350+
Marketing freelance rates guide	
Freelance level	**Daily fee band**
Account executive or Marketing assistant	£100–150
Senior account executive/ Marketing executive to Account manager	£130–200
Account director or Marketing manager	£180–250
Associate director or Marketing director	£250–400+
Editorial freelance rates guide	
Freelance level	**Daily fee band**
Subeditor or Staff writer	£110–140
Web editor or Junior copywriter	£140–180
Mid-weight copywriter or Journalist	£180–220
Advertising copywriter or Editorial director	£250+

Source Xchangeteam Group Limited

TV freelance rates guide

Inland Revenue has demarcated the TV world by having strict regulations dictating who can freelance in TV and who can't. For example, cameramen and editors are always freelance. TV freelance rates are very transparent, relatively fixed and are usually quoted as weekly fees.

Freelance level	**Weekly fee band**
Production director	£1,100
Series producer	£1,250–1,300
Assistant producer	£800
Researcher	£500–600
Production manager	£800–900
Production coordinator	£450

Source Ricochet

Interim management rates guide

Interim level	Daily fee band
CEO, MD, functional Executive Director of a large multi-national	£1,500–3,000
CEO, MD, functional Executive Director of a medium/large multi-national	£1,000–1,800
General Manager, Divisional MD, MD, functional Head of a medium-sized national/international business	£900–1,200
General Manager, functional Head of a small business	£750–1,000
Senior manager	£600–900

Source Boyden Interim Management Limited

IT freelance rates guide

Freelance level	Daily fee band
CTO/CIO	£400+
IT director/Head of IT	£270–540
IT manager/Chief engineer	£115–270
IT support team leader/Supervisor	£90–115
IT support engineer/Analyst	£85–90

Source: IT recruitment websites

On the other hand, freelance consultants selling a skill that is more readily available have less control over their rates and will generally bow to market pressures. Their rates for longer assignments are usually lower than the rates they charge for short assignments. They are also likely to soften their demands if you are able to promise them regular work in the future, if you can offer them projects that are of particular interest, or if they are just starting out on their freelance career.

Remember that the first rule of negotiation is to achieve a win-win situation for all those involved. This is particularly important if you hope to establish a productive, long-term relationship with any freelance consultant. So be fair!

If a freelance consultant consistently produces excellent results for your organisation, you might also consider paying him or her a retainer fee as a way of securing your claim to his or her expertise. Conversely, some organisations pay retainers to keep highly regarded freelance consultants *out* of the marketplace. So although they may not need the freelancer all the time, they do not want their competitors to use him or her at any time. Other organisations pay freelance consultants success bonuses. This may involve paying a slightly lower fee towards the start of an assignment, offsetting this with larger payments to reward loyalty and commitment throughout the lifetime of a project or to reward particular success. An increasing number of consultancies use specialised, well-connected freelance consultants to work on new business drives and pay commission on any new business the campaign generates.

Understandably, a freelance consultant is likely to charge more if required to work at weekends and/or over public holidays. Whereas some freelance consultants charge overtime for long hours, others assume that any project will include some overtime, and build an element of goodwill into their rates accordingly. Yet others may negotiate. As a rule, the higher the basic rate, the fewer additional payments a freelance consultant will seek. At the same time, be aware that freelance consultants may become resentful if they feel they are being exploited. It is important, therefore, to agree your position up front and when further negotiation might be appropriate.

Agree what expenses are payable and establish whether or not your freelance consultant is VAT registered. You will also need to factor into your figures, your freelance resourcing agency fees.

Include a contingency cost in your final budget. Be prepared to renegotiate costs if there are unforeseen changes to your brief or timescales.

EXPLAIN INVOICING/PAYMENT PROCEDURES

Having established whether you are paying by the assignment, the week, the day or the hour, agree how often the freelancer should invoice you. For example: is the assignment long enough to warrant interim payments?

Freelance consultants are often self-employed and a healthy cash flow is essential to keeping them positive and focused. They do not have the resources of a large organisation, and quite simply, their invoice is their livelihood. If your organisation fails to pay its invoices on time, freelancers can lose motivation and become disenchanted – even resentful. In the interests of fostering goodwill and harmonious working relationships, consider making special arrangements to ensure that your accounts department pays freelance invoices with minimum delay according to whatever terms you have agreed. You may agree to pay a freelance consultant part of his or her fee up front or on a monthly retainer basis – especially if there is a high demand for his or her services.

Bear in mind that not all freelance consultants submit invoices directly. In some cases, they may be on your payroll or on the payroll of the agency that placed them with you. Individual circumstances will vary, but ensure that you are clear about a freelance consultant's employment status and terms of business before the assignment starts.

TIMESHEETS/LOGGING PROCEDURES

Completing timesheets is generally the preserve of those freelance consultants who are paid on a time basis via your payroll or your freelance resourcing agency's payroll. This section is therefore irrelevant if you are buying a product or service from a freelance consultant based on a fixed fee, because you would agree a price for his or her products or services, regardless of how long it takes to deliver. In the case of self-employed consultants who are charging on a 'time' basis, they would submit an invoice rather than complete a timesheet. But they will log the number of days worked with both their client and, if applicable, their freelance resourcing agency, to ensure that all parties agree on the amount of time to be billed. This is the 'currency' of the project.

Logging days worked and completing timesheets can be laborious. Freelance consultants often find the chore particularly laborious because they have to stay on top of three systems – their own, their client's and their freelance resourcing agency's. However, if the project fee is determined by time, you need to receive timely and accurate records from them. Conveniently, many freelance consultants can only invoice once they have submitted records, which makes compliance with your procedures somewhat easier to enforce.

But the fact that many freelancers also work remotely is another factor that can compromise record-keeping. The secret is to ensure that your internal systems are set up to make it as easy as possible for freelancers to comply with your procedures at all times, regardless of where they are based. Many organisations now have online logging timesheet systems that are accessible via the Internet from anywhere. Others use simple email-based systems.

AGREE WORKING PLACE AND MODUS OPERANDI

Should the freelance consultant work on his or her own site, on your site or at a client site? Should he or she work from a combination of locations? If so, how and when? The answers will depend on numerous factors. For example, does the freelance consultant require regular meetings with your other staff? If so, it makes sense for them to work near each other. On the other hand, if the freelance consultant is completing a self-contained piece of work that does not involve other people, he or she is likely to be more productive in his or her own workplace – provided there is access there to all the technology and/or equipment required.

Increasingly sophisticated and mobile technology means that many workers – knowledge workers in particular – no longer need to work from a specific location. A recent survey in *Human Resources* magazine (September, 2005) says that the falling cost and rising availability of technology explains why nearly three-quarters of businesses now offer remote or home working as an option.

Ultimately, everyone involved must be comfortable when agreeing where and how a freelance consultant should work, and any agreement should reflect the nature of the assignment.

INTRODUCE YOUR CULTURE

Before your freelance consultants begin work, familiarise them with your organisation's internal culture. If they understand the context of their assignment and the environment they will be working in, they are less likely to end up working in a vacuum. During the familiarisation process, it may become apparent that the freelance consultant is incompatible with your culture and any relationship is doomed to failure. Discovering this before the assignment begins saves time, money – and goodwill.

AGREE ANY ADDITIONAL RESOURCES

Consider what other resources – if any – a freelance consultant might need to complete an assignment. Will it be necessary to provide office space, equipment, IT hardware/software, admin support, tools, people, etc? Be aware that providing additional support could have tax implications for your organisation and the freelance consultant. This is because any additional support might imply that you have an employer–employee relationship rather than a business-to-business relationship. We address this issue in more detail in Chapter 6.

AGREE REPORTING LINES, APPROVAL PROCESSES, AUTHORITY LEVELS

Who does the freelance consultant answer to – and who answers to the freelance consultant? Who does the freelance consultant report to and/or work with? Who should he or she include in the communication loop – and at what stage?

Other questions to address include: who has sign-off authority over a freelance consultant's work, and when is their approval required? It is not unusual to find that freelance consultants – especially project managers – are responsible for handling substantial budgets running into millions of pounds. Often, freelance consultants in this position can raise purchase orders but require sign-off from the finance department before assuming full budgetary control of the project. But what processes are in place to ensure that they exercise their authority ethically and transparently?

As for authority levels, these vary widely – from freelance consultants engaged at CEO level to those working solo and independently of the client structures. The former will have full authority over the organisation. But just like permanently employed CEOs, they will be accountable to a board of directors and, ultimately, its chairman. Solo workers, on the other hand, are often accountable to a single person within the client organisation.

It is not always necessary to assign authority explicitly. There are times, for example, when a freelance consultant's specialist skills and knowledge give him or her implicit authority over your staff. The challenge facing the freelance consultant is to win people's respect as a trusted adviser. After that, you are free to agree what level of authority he or she should have and over whom. Ultimately, if a freelance consultant is respected, he or she will have authority.

ADDRESS CONFIDENTIALITY/INTELLECTUAL PROPERTY/CLIENT CONTACT ISSUES

Moving from client to client, assignment to assignment may be a freelance consultant's prerogative. But you need to consider how their mobility might impact on the interests of your organisation. Confidentiality and intellectual property (IP) are issues of particular importance – especially if a freelance consultant is involved in pitching and business development. This area is a fertile ground for ideas and innovation – two factors that are critical to sustaining an organisation's competitive edge.

While you don't want to lose out on the benefits a freelance consultant might bring you, you must also be realistic about protecting your own interests. At the same time, it is reassuring that reputable freelance consultants invariably take the issue of confidentiality as seriously as you do. If they fail to respect your interests, they run the risk of compromising their reputation – and losing business. Furthermore, many freelance consultants can correctly point out that loyalty is not a virtue confined to the permanent payroll. Indeed, it is not unusual to find freelance consultants who have been with an organisation longer than some of its permanent employees. Current research estimates that the average tenure among CEOs, for example, is just two years.

We recommend that confidentiality and IP issues should be covered by the standard contract you sign with freelance consultants – a matter that we address in more detail in Chapter 6.

Contact between the hirer's clients and freelance consultants is another potentially sensitive and complex area – although this applies to a limited number of organisations, primarily service organisations such as consultancies. Some consultancies are more flexible than others when it comes to freelance consultants' dealing directly with their clients. Many worry that clients will object to dealing with someone who is not part of the consultancy's core team. The truth is that many clients draw reassurance from the fact that their interests are being served by a specialist working as part of a dedicated team. Ironically, a growing number of organisations hire freelance consultants to handle their consultancy relationships. And, of course, some freelance consultants are hired specifically for their client handling skills.

To avoid confusion and uncertainty in this area, agree your boundaries and expectations before the assignment starts and set them according to the nature of the project. As a general guide, it is advisable not to make a freelance consultant your only point of contact with a client.

EXPLAIN IT/HEALTH AND SAFETY/ENVIRONMENTAL/ETHICAL POLICIES

When it comes to business-critical management policies, brief freelance consultants as thoroughly as you brief your permanent staff. In certain sectors, freelance consultants have a legal obligation to provide formal evidence that they understand your policies and are complying with them. Rules will vary, but ensure that you remain up to date with current legislation and regulatory requirements. Also ensure that your freelance consultant has sufficient insurance in place to meet all regulatory requirements. This is especially important where professional indemnity insurance is concerned – see Chapter 6.

AGREE EVALUATION PROCEDURES

It is important that a freelance consultant is comfortable with the way his or her work will be judged – and when. Evaluation does not have take to place at the end of an assignment. On the contrary, regular evaluation throughout is an effective way of focusing people and resources.

Essentially, there are two types of evaluation, although in some cases they may converge:

- *Evaluating freelance consultants*
  Did they deliver what I wanted? Did they meet the objectives? Were they integral to the success of the project? Did I enjoy working with them? Do they fit into our culture? Are they easy to communicate with? What are their strengths and weaknesses? Are they hardworking, and did they go the extra mile?

- *Evaluating the project*
  Did the project meet its objectives and have the desired outcomes? What worked well, and what could have been done better?

The evaluation option you choose will vary according to your pre-agreed objectives and the complexity of the assignment. While it may be relatively easy, for example, to evaluate the success of a one-off client survey, evaluating the success of a long-term campaign to transform an organisation's corporate mindset may be far less objective and finite. Whereas pragmatism should decide the evaluation method, ensure that everyone agrees which one to use.

In practice, evaluation is frequently subjective, often verbal, and comes from the person responsible for hiring the freelance consultant. However, this form of evaluation should be supported by formal feedback mechanisms such as questionnaires. If the freelance consultant has integrated closely with your organisation, ask for feedback or testimonials from the people he or she interacted with most frequently. They might include project team members, clients and suppliers among others. The list will vary, but aim to build up a 360-degree perspective. If the freelance consultant works independently of your organisation providing a product or service, it makes more sense to gather feedback on the quality of those products or services from the people who use them.

KNOWLEDGE TRANSFER

Capturing lessons and transferring skills are vital to deriving maximum value from freelance consultants – but these issues are often overlooked. Freelance consultants can provide interesting insights into your organisation and the way it functions, and their objective feedback can help to raise your organisation's performance.

There are various ways to capture their feedback. Ideally, you should agree on the most suitable method before the freelance consultant starts work. The simplest option is to meet the freelance consultant at the end of the assignment to analyse the highs and lows of the project. Alternatively, you might ask the freelance consultant to submit a written report on his or her experience of your organisation once he or she has completed the assignment. If an assignment has gone particularly well, a report can be a useful way of linking the freelance consultant to your organisation for further assignments. If the assignment has not gone well, a written report is an effective post-mortem tool.

As the assignment progresses, take steps to transfer the freelance consultant's knowledge to your own organisation. This is particularly important if the freelance consultant is a specialist in a particular field with skills that your staff do not have.

EXIT MANAGEMENT

As Nick Robeson, chairman of the Interim Management Association, points out:

It is important to recognise when it is time for a freelance consultant to leave. This can be a difficult decision, especially if the freelance consultant has performed well. If you have a legitimate project to complete and the person in question has the skills to complete it, that is one thing. But keeping someone on board as a sort of comfort-blanket is another thing altogether.

One of the difficulties that Nick Robeson identifies is 'assignment drift'. This develops when a freelance consultant remains in an organisation because he or she has been effective in the past but is no longer working on a specific project managed according to the guidelines laid down in this chapter. A freelancer in this situation can rapidly turn from a highly effective resource into an unproductive liability. Clearly, 'assignment drift' benefits nobody. It is therefore important to agree terms of reference and an end date, and to communicate regularly to ensure that the assignment is on track.

Failure to manage exits can also lead to 'mission creep', by which a freelance consultant's contract is continually extended. This is not necessarily a problem, but it must be managed closely. Extending a contract could make sense if the hiring organisation is keen to secure first rights to a freelance consultant's talent. But the arrangement may not suit a results-focused freelancer in search of variety and new challenges. So before the original assignment ends, discuss whether extending the contract is likely to be in everybody's interests.

A handover period is essential to managing the exit process effectively. Freelance consultants can play an invaluable part in recruiting, mentoring and training a permanent employee to replace them. During the handover it often makes sense for the freelance consultant to work alongside the replacement over a number of weeks, gradually reducing his or her hours as the departure date approaches. Before the freelance consultant finally leaves, it is important to establish who is going to manage his or her legacy. This is particularly important if the freelancer has been involved in any type of change programme. After all, it is vital to ensure that the changes he or she has set in motion are correctly implemented to support an organisation's long-term objectives.

ON DAY 1

Induction checklist for Day 1 of an interim assignment

Client name:	
Contact: *Title:* *Telephone number:* *email address:*	
Location: *web address:*	
Introduced by:	
Who do I meet?	
BACKGROUND INFORMATION	

KEY OBJECTIVES   *1*
               2
               3	

KEY OUTPUTS
    Presentation
    Report
 	
    Day-to-day management of
    the team	

REQUIREMENTS
    Number of days:
    Timescale:
 	
Daily rate:	

KEY PERSONNEL *Organisation chart* *Line manager:* *Senior people:* *Influences:*	

IT Web address: Telephone number: email address: Training:	
Updates/regular meetings: who with? how often?	
STAFF:	
Date:	Name:
First day Office checklist	Telephone system Business cards Stationery Password email address Telephone number Fax no. Information/Reception IT help client number Office help desk number
First day HR checklist	Induction Security ID pass Policies and procedures

Source: Janet Morris, interim marketing consultant

By now, we have established that the three essentials underpinning the successful management of freelance consultants are preparation, preparation and preparation. Laying solid foundations is vital to forming a mutually productive relationship based on communication and trust. This process will begin during the preparation phase and it is vital to continue it from Day 1 of the assignment.

Be pragmatic when introducing freelance consultants to their new working environment. Some level of induction will help a freelance consultant to feel welcome and comfortable with practical issues such as security and how to access the computer system. In some instances it may also be necessary for the freelance consultant to undergo some level of training. Ultimately, any induction process should be tailored to give the freelance consultant whatever information he or she needs to set to work with minimum delay.

On page 120 above, we have included an induction checklist produced by Janet Morris, an interim marketing consultant, who developed it to help her clients improve the way that they induct a freelance consultant. It includes many of the points you may wish to cover with your freelance consultants on Day 1.

PART 2: WORKING IN PARTNERSHIP

Having established a clear framework at the beginning of the relationship, getting the best from freelance consultants is essentially about nurturing a positive two-way relationship with them in pursuit of shared objectives. This relationship should be exactly the same sort of relationship you would aim to build with any valued business partner. Treat it as a business-to-business relationship rather than an employer–employee relationship. In other words, gear your management approach to maximising immediate performance and achieving results.

THE FOUR PRINCIPLES OF SUCCESSFUL FREELANCE MANAGEMENT

Trust, open communication and clarity are vital from the start of your relationship. Once you begin working together, the emphasis should be on motivation, delegation, collaboration and accountability – the four principles of successful freelance management.

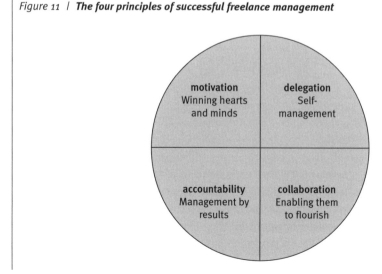

Figure 11 I **The four principles of successful freelance management**

Motivation

As the skills shortage continues to bite, organisations cannot afford to take talent for granted. That is why it is so important to sell your organisation and its vision with passion and conviction. So get your first-choice freelance consultants excited about working on your project. It could make the difference between winning their buy-in – or losing them to a competitor. Making them feel a part of the team throughout the assignment will help motivate them to achieve your target results. Freelance consultants are very conscious that they are only as good as their last job. Tapping into this awareness with the promise of a glowing reference is a very effective way of sustaining their motivation.

Furthermore, freelance communities tend to be close knit. So if you establish an exciting reputation for offering high-quality work, you are creating a virtuous circle which will make it easier to attract high-quality freelance talent in the future.

Geoff Nicol, who heads up Navyblue, a strategic communications group, has firm views on the importance of motivation. 'The moment a freelance consultant begins working for me, they cease to be a freelance consultant,' he says. 'Regardless of how long you hire them for, it's essential to make them feel that they're part of your team from the start. Making people feel indispensable is the key to getting the best out of them – and freelance consultants prove the rule.'

There is, however, a parallel argument that freelance consultants are a good thing precisely because they do not make any demands on your motivational skills. 'Freelance consultants are essentially business people. Most of them happen to be one-man bands,' says the academic and author Professor Richard Scase, currently Professor of Organisational Behaviour at the University of Kent at Canterbury. 'They are solely responsible for keeping their business on the road. What stronger motivation can there be?'

Richard Baines, director of the London-based HR consultancy Argyll HR, offers a third perspective:

> *Expecting a freelance consultant to work miracles under their own direction can be a recipe for failure. With the right motivation and handling, however, they can add real value to many parts of an organisation.*

Few organisations would dispute the fundamental importance of wining hearts and minds when it comes to motivating their permanent employees. Many back this understanding with extensive investment of time, money and resources. But most of this investment excludes freelance consultants. This may be intentional. After all, we have already established that a degree of detachment between client and freelancer is often desirable. But we would also argue that selling your organisation and your project to freelance consultants is essential to creating a sound working relationship with them and maximising the returns on your investment in them – even if that relationship only lasts for as long as the assignment.

Delegation

Experience demonstrates that it is increasingly difficult to motivate people or inspire solutions by imposing top-down management. This is particularly true in the case of freelance consultants, who typically reject command-and-control management in favour of delegation.

The ability to self-manage is one of the strengths that defines good freelance consultants. You have hired them on the strength of their track record and their expertise, and they will expect the freedom to apply that expertise within an agreed framework to achieve your target results. In other words: delegate to them. They will certainly not appreciate being micro-managed, supervised or stifled by bureaucracy.

To sustain a productive relationship with a freelance consultant, you need to understand that his or her mindset is different from the mindset of a permanent employee. As we explained in Chapter 1, freelance consultants share a common DNA with common strengths. They are invariably highly motivated, well organised and very energetic. Their talent for innovation springs from a capacity for asking awkward questions and challenging the status quo. Rather than getting hung up on status and hierarchies, they are goal-oriented and self-motivated to achieve results. Such focused and capable personalities are far more responsive to decentralisation than command and control, and it is important to adapt your management style accordingly. As knowledge workers, freelance consultants prefer a management style that empowers them to add value through their talent.

Collaboration

The growing emphasis on partnership with freelance consultants aligns with the general shift towards collaboration between everyone in the workplace. In Chapter 8 we examine how this shift is likely to shape the future of work – both permanent and freelance. It is already clear that teamworking has become an important feature of working life in the UK. In *Working in the Twenty-First Century* (Economic Research Council, 2005), Michael Moynagh and Richard Worsley cite research that shows that one in three workplaces is increasing the use of formal teams, and hardly any are moving in the opposite direction.

Collaborating with freelance consultants as business partners gives them the freedom and confidence to flourish. Your role is as their 'enabler' or 'mentor'. Establish what tools they need to achieve the results you require, then support them with guidance on the complexities of your organisation's culture, people and politics so that they are able to be successful. Work with the freelance consultant to identify any potential barriers, and agree strategies for the freelance consultant to overcome them.

This trend towards collaborative networks in the workplace fits neatly with the freelance model. Organisations that value teamworking among permanent employees are often the most accomplished at unlocking the value of freelance talent through effective integration and management.

The trend towards collaborative working is also evidenced by the proliferation of online and offline professional networks, where freelance consultants thrive in an environment that favours empowerment through decentralisation of authority. Results prevail over process. It is this environment that you should aim to foster through your relationships with the freelance community.

Accountability

Managing by results is the key to managing freelance consultants effectively – provided both parties are clear about your objectives and expectations. When it comes to making freelance consultants accountable, appeal to their sense of self-discipline rather than solely relying on external measures. Clearly, the ultimate sanction at your disposal is terminating your contract with the freelance consultants – or simply not asking them back.

Credible freelance consultants understand their own strengths and weaknesses and set their standards accordingly. Playing to their strengths determines which assignments they take on and which assignments they turn down. They recognise that self-discipline and self-directed learning are vital to meeting their own standards, and they are acutely aware of failing to meet them. In other words, you are less likely to find yourself in a position where you have to tell a freelance consultant when or how to improve his or her performance. But if one does fail to meet the required standard, ensure that you have a process in place to terminate your relationship.

Focusing on results means adapting the level of supervision and red tape you apply to the freelance consultant while adjusting the extent to which he or she integrates with your organisation. Integration is not always necessary to achieve your target results and a degree of detachment from your organisation can actually be beneficial.

Because freelance consultants are often specialists in their own fields, they often know more about their work than the person who is expected to manage them. Indeed, there are times when they are specifically asked to manage aspects of their client's own organisation. In these cases it is important that the client has absolute trust in the freelance consultant's track record and reputation. After all, detailed supervision of specialists is unrealistic. Instead, high-calibre freelance consultants should be free to work with greater autonomy – provided they ultimately deliver the results you agreed with them.

Key point summary

- Aim to establish a business-to-business relationship with freelance consultants, not an employment relationship.
- Establish an open, transparent relationship based on trust.
- Invest time up front in getting the framework right.
- The framework should be discussed in detail before the assignment begins. It should address: objectives, deliverables, timescales/milestones, start date, trial

period, early termination, costs, invoicing/payment, timesheets, working place and modus operandi, culture, additional resources, authority levels, legals, company policies, evaluation, knowledge transfer, and exit.

- The four principles of getting the best from freelance consultants are motivation, delegation, collaboration and accountability.

8

The future of freelancing

INTRODUCTION: THE REVOLUTION IS OVER – LONG LIVE THE REVOLUTION

Perhaps the most radical conclusion we have drawn from our research is that the future belongs to those organisations with the vision and skill to treat all staff as freelance consultants – regardless of whether they are permanent or temporary, new or experienced, senior or junior, skilled or non-skilled. Tomorrow's workers will all think like freelancers, whatever their employment status

Emma Brierley, founder of London-based freelance resourcing agency Xchangeteam Group

Towards the end of the 1990s, the air was thick with revolution. Offices, conference halls, gastropubs and the media were alive with rumours that the end of the workplace as we knew it was nigh. Hot desks were about to replace offices. Virtual organisations were set to proliferate like mushrooms. Employees were all set to reject jobs for life in favour of financially and spiritually enriching self-employment. Armed with a mobile phone and a laptop with Internet access, they could now work when and where it suited them in pursuit of the perfect work–life balance. For a while, tomorrow's world belonged to the self-actualising freelance consultant.

By 2015, I predict that 30 per cent of the workforce will be working in non-permanent jobs. Right now, all employers should be taking steps to incorporate the use of freelance consultants into their human resource strategy.

Professor Richard Scase, Professor of Organisational Behaviour, University of Kent at Canterbury

According to some.

To others, the freelance revolution was always a triumph of hype over reality with no more substance or credibility than a dotcom bubble. It was, say some observers, largely confined to a small number of high-profile, highly articulate individuals with positions of influence in the creative and technology industries – and friends in the media willing to present their personal aspirations as universal truths. It was only their talent for talking up the freelance lifestyle that transformed it from a demographic flicker into the next big thing.

Hourglass model calls time on middle managers

David Coats, deputy director of research at the Work Foundation, argues strongly that statistics simply do not support the theory that the freelance model will dominate the workplaces of the future.

Instead, he argues that workplace demographics are beginning to resemble the shape of an hourglass. In the middle, there is a steady thinning of middle-range, medium-skilled, white-collar workers as trends such as offshoring and automation begin to make their mark. Above and below the thinning core there is an expansion of high-skilled and low-skilled jobs respectively.

Some argue that the hourglass model will benefit freelance consultants more than any other group. As the middle of the hourglass continues to hollow out, the freelance community will be the first to pick up the fall-out. Others argue that professional and affluent workers at the top of the glass will simply buy personal services from people on low pay at the bottom – bypassing freelance consultants. But the obvious counter-argument swings back in favour of freelance consultants. With thriving businesses, they will join those at the top of the hourglass buying personal services from those at the bottom.

One way or the other, there is a consensus that it is those in the middle of the hourglass who remain most vulnerable to the trends that we examine in this book. The question is: will they trade up or down?

Inevitably, perhaps, the truth lies somewhere between these two positions. In the cold light of the new millennium, a more subtle and complex picture is emerging. Some commentators cite statistics that show that the explosive rise in the number of self-employed workers has simply not materialised. Then again, commentators such as the academic and author Charles Handy argue that the statistics are not telling the whole truth.

'Statistics claim that 90 per cent of the UK workforce is permanent,' Handy reminds us. 'But of this total, 24 per cent of the workers are part-time, 13 per cent are self-employed, 8 per cent work for limited companies with no employees. In other words, they are freelance. These figures add up to a strange sort of permanence.'

In Handy's opinion, it is in the interests of the authorities to suggest that the workplace will be dominated by a large permanent workforce for the foreseeable future. 'It gives the feeling that the world is secure and predictable. People know their place in it. Governments can collect money from it more easily. But the reality,' declares Handy, 'is that already over half of the workforce are not in "proper" jobs.'

Future trends – **Broadcasters lead demand for freelance talent**

The BBC currently outsources 25 per cent of its production to external independents. The opening of its Window of Creative Competition (WOCC) initiative means that this figure is set to grow. In future, a further 25 per cent of production will be up for grabs between in-house BBC teams and independents. Channel 4 has always outsourced and will continue to do so while ITV will probably continue with a mix of solutions. This will result in higher demand for freelance consultants across the broadcasting sector.

BLURRING THE DISTINCTIONS BETWEEN PERMANENT AND FREELANCE

This debate promises to run as long as *The Mousetrap* without necessarily reaching the play's neat resolutions. But through the swirl of conflicting views and statistics, our own research confirmed a number of certainties. It became clear, for example, that social, demographic and economic trends – accelerated by increasingly powerful and accessible communication technology – mean that freelance consultants will become increasingly important players in the labour market. Later in this chapter we examine these trends in some depth.

But perhaps the most radical conclusion we have drawn from our research is that the future belongs to those organisations with the vision and skill to treat all staff as freelance consultants – regardless of whether they are permanent or temporary, new or experienced, senior or junior, skilled or non-skilled.

This finding clearly has profound implications for the way organisations manage their human resources. For a start, future success will depend on how successfully management is able to implement the processes and systems covered in previous chapters. But implementing processes and systems could well be the easy part. Long-term, the toughest challenge involves bringing about a change of management culture by replacing traditional management tactics with a more enlightened and freelance-friendly mindset. The differences between old and new are clear:

Traditional line managers

- favour command and control
- value status
- avoid risk.

Freelance-friendly managers

- are results- and goal-oriented
- recognise the value of teamworking/networking
- dismiss status and hierarchy.

In October 2005, the *Times* reported figures from the Office for National Statistics stating that 90 per cent of homeworkers are in managerial, professional, technical and skilled jobs. Many are self-employed, around two-thirds are men, and the trend is growing among older employees. Most report that working away from the office boosts their productivity, sharpens their focus and delivers results. The problem is that their superiors continue to inhibit the homeworking trend. According to the report, many managers find it difficult to move on from the traditional command-and-control mindset, which dictates that everyone must be seen to be working in the office. The perception that people are skiving if they are offsite remains prevalent. If the *Times* is correct, arguments in favour of the freelance model have a long way to go.

PUTTING FUTURE CHALLENGES IN CURRENT CONTEXT

Personal predictions – Tom Peters

In his recent book *Re-imagine! Business excellence in a disruptive age* (Dorling Kindersley, 2003), business management guru Tom Peters compared patterns of change in today's corporate sector to established patterns of change in the US military (see Table 7 below). His conclusion? The change in both sectors produces very similar results.

Table 7 | *Patterns of change in corporate culture*

Yesterday's corporate culture	Tomorrow's corporate culture
'Old economy' army	'New economy' army
Steep, bureaucratic, with lots of 'brass'	Flat, decentralised, with limited 'brass'
Slow but sure	Fast and sure
Heavy, therefore lethal	Light, but no less lethal
Overwhelming force, difficult to manoeuvre	Precision munitions, able to 'turn on a dime'
Biggest guns in town	Smartest systems on Earth
Soldiers in massed formation, riding in tanks and towing heavy artillery	Units of five or ten soldiers, armed mostly with technology, able to call remotely upon an array of armaments
Firepower-intense	Information-intense
Hierarchical, with independent units that relate through top-down command-and-control operations	Network-centric, with interdependent groups that engage in ad-hoc operational planning
Lots of friction, low co-ordination – especially with other armed services and with Government agencies	Friction-free, open communication – both within units and across organisational divisions
Very 'real'	Very 'virtual'

John Knell, formerly Director of Research at the Work Foundation, is a director and co-founder of the Intelligence Agency ideas consultancy. In his view, the argument has already been won.

An increasing number of organisations now operate in ways that match the freelance model – regardless of whether or not they actually use freelance consultants. Demand is unpredictable, response times are shorter, deadlines are punishing. In this scenario, flexibility is of the essence. Even within the most traditional organisations, teamworking is becoming the norm.

Cautions Knell,

A team-based organisation will always need a stable core, but to meet demand, they must bring together people with the optimum balance of skills for a defined period of time to deliver against a specific set of objectives before disbanding. Whether team members pick up a regular salary check or not, every employee is now expected to think and act like a freelancer. It has become an unwritten law of the workplace.

But other commentators and experts we interviewed expressed little optimism that typical employers were in a position to do so. Indeed, some commentators were positively pessimistic. Charles Handy predicts that the large organisations, which he describes as 'elephants', need to change their act – and fast.

Personal predictions – Richard Baines, director of London-based human resources consultancy Argyll HR

'If current trends continue,' predicts Richard, 'the split between project-based contracts and retainer agreements could eventually reach 50/50. This will have a profound impact on the relationship between freelance consultants, the organisations that employ them and the agencies that place them. With timescales becoming even tighter and demand for freelance consultants growing, it is simply not possible to find the right freelancer for the job at the drop of a hat. As a result, we could begin to see organisations developing retainer-style relationships with a roster of tried and tested freelance consultants. Who knows? We might even see organisations engaging agencies on a retainer basis to secure a reliable supply of freelance talent.'

'Instead of exploiting the freelance mindset, too many managers still run their businesses like factories, where the organisation or its shareholders own the means of production: intellectual property,' says Handy. 'But in the knowledge economy, intellectual property belongs to people who come up with the ideas. At present, most of us are content to exchange our intellectual property for a salary and the promise of a permanent job. Soon, this decision will be dismissed as crazy.'

Future trends – Actors, authors . . . and now freelance consultants

As people become aware that their knowledge or talents have a marketable value, they will be reluctant to sell it for a salary. They will want to charge a fee or a royalty, or receive a percentage of the profits. Increasingly, they will negotiate individual contracts via their agent or lawyer. What is already the norm for actors and even for authors will become standard practice in the freelance community.

Instead, argues Handy, the sharpest innovators will opt out of permanent employment, develop their ideas and sell them back to the people who used to employ them – and become richer in the process. Smart organisations will recognise that they cannot play Canute in the face of change and they will go with the flow. Rather than swimming against the freelance tide, they will reshape their culture, processes and structures to unlock their value.

Personal predictions – Antoine Lever, Commercial Director, Omniis Limited

In Antoine Lever's opinion, the UK workforce will gradually be made up of more and more people working on a non-permanent basis. 'Low-skilled jobs are going to be offshored; high-skilled people are going to choose to sell their services to a range of companies at premium rates while achieving greater work–lifestyle balance,' he predicts. 'Companies will benefit from this way of working because they will be able to minimise overheads and source the best possible team to fit their projects.' What's more, adds Antoine, technology has now progressed to the stage where it can support this vision.

But as Handy reminds us, elephants don't change quickly. Many organisations are still staffed by people who value status above results and buy into the illusion of long-term job security in a world where jobs-for-life have all but vanished.

However, attitudes among young people coming onto the job market are markedly different. Brought up to embrace technology rather than fear it, this generation is unlikely to tolerate the constraints imposed by its elders. On the contrary, these young people are more concerned about taking control of their own destinies by striking out on their own, moving from project to project guided only by their personal interests and creative instincts.

Introducing globule management

'Younger people respond better to "globule management",' notes Handy. He has coined the term 'globule management' to describe the way in which fluid, multi-skilled and cross-disciplinary teams solidify within an organisation around specific projects for finite periods. These teams typically comprise a mixture of permanent employees and freelance consultants who unite behind a set of shared objectives. The purpose is to build small units in which everyone knows everybody else's strengths and weaknesses. Once those objectives are achieved, team members disperse in search of new challenges.

According to the globule management model, organisations will no longer be able to hang on to intellectual property, exploiting it on their terms. Rather, their role is to manage how other people's intellectual property is delivered to the consumer. This demands a facilitating infrastructure comprising schedulers, buyers, advisers and managers who are expected to manage processes – not people. If you are looking for an example, just think Nike. Directors will be responsible to the people who own the intellectual property, not shareholders.

Whether or not the globule management concept becomes a reality, most of the people we interviewed agree that change is inevitable, even though it is likely to be gradual. 'We've already come a long way,' says Handy.

> There are those who use statistics to prove that the status quo prevails. But you need to be very careful about what statistics conceal as well as reveal. There are figures that state 10 million people in the UK are economically inactive. But you can bet they are active. In fact, most of them are likely to be portfolio workers. According to the figures, 8 per cent or 2 million UK organisations have no employees in this country. Another 2 million have between one and four employees. Incorporating themselves into organisations conceals the fact that these people are freelance. It makes them invisible to the authorities. I refer to them as independent workers and they are pioneering a new attitude to work.

IDENTIFYING THE TRENDS, WEIGHING THE ARGUMENTS

Handy argues a compelling case, but so do many of the commentators on the other side of the debating chamber. To weigh the arguments and draw your own conclusions, it is important to examine the trends that are already shaping tomorrow's working practices.

In their recent book *Working in the Twenty-First Century* (Economic Research Council, 2005), Michael Moynagh and Richard Worsley identify four key themes for the next 20 years, all of which seem likely to reinforce the strength of the freelance proposition.

Workplaces will be transformed as the UK economy moves up the value chain. In the face of intensifying competition from Asia, Eastern Europe and elsewhere, say the authors, UK companies will be forced to produce increasingly sophisticated products and develop new ones.

As a result,

> the workplace will be an arena of constant change as new processes are introduced, technology becomes more advanced, workers are retrained, new forms of organisation emerge and new management techniques are developed.

Change will be more dramatic in how people work than in how they are employed. People will need to become steadily more flexible in the way they work and flexible working practices will become vital to an organisation's efficiency. Mobile working will become more prevalent as people use mobile technology to work in transit between destinations.

The boundaries between life inside and outside work will grow more fluid, resulting in people working longer hours on an informal basis.

The steady progress towards mobile working over the last 20 years has already left its mark on the way we work. According to Moynagh and Worsley, in 2002 almost 3.8 million people (13.4 per cent) worked either mainly in their own home, or mainly in different places using home as a base, or mainly elsewhere with at least one full day at home. 'This was a startling jump on the near 3 million (11.3 per cent) who were working in these ways a mere five years earlier.' As the authors point out, what has increased is not so much homeworking as people working in multiple centres and on the move. They conclude: 'The conventional workplace as a centre for employment is being chipped away.'

As people are given more choice in where they work, some organisations may struggle to strike a workable balance between decentralisation and appropriate central control. *Managing this tension will remain a dominant theme, and will give rise to a variety of organisational forms*. This is yet another factor that favours freelance working.

New motivational techniques by management will gradually transform the experience of work. According to the authors: 'Managers will seek new methods of control as they give workers more autonomy. Increasingly, attention will focus on winning commitment so that workers want to achieve the organisation's goals.' Once again, these are the conditions in which the freelance mindset thrives.

BUILDING AN EVEN MORE COMPELLING ARGUMENT

Our own views and experience align strongly with the thrust of Moynagh and Worsley's arguments above. We have also identified several supporting arguments in favour of the freelance model.

An expanding global economy

Evidence suggests that the global economy is on the brink of a dramatic expansion, the World Bank projecting 40 per cent growth between now and 2015. The UK economy is well placed to take advantage of this expansion as business booms in areas where the country excels. Likely growth sectors include pharmaceuticals, business services such as accounting and legal work, health and education, hi-tech manufacturing, and earnings from rights, royalties, licence payments, etc – all high-value parts of the knowledge economy.

This is backed up by Professor Scase, who predicts that freelance consultants are here to stay. 'A supply of reliable, flexible talent is essential to the future of all knowledge-based economies,' he says. 'And Britain epitomises the knowledge-based economy.'

If it materialises, the economic boom is likely to exacerbate the UK's chronic skills shortage, especially in London and the south-east. In response, organisations will explore new sources of talent. These will include older people, immigrants, women with children – and freelance consultants.

The influence of women in the workplace cannot be under-estimated. They already make up almost half of the UK workforce. In 11 per cent of couples, women are breaking into more senior positions and earning more than their partner. In 2004, 44.1 per cent of the 13 million women in employment worked part-time against only 10.6 per cent of men. In future, women will attain even greater academic heights and also expect to combine work and children.

Work will make even greater demands on everyone in the workplace, male or female. In turn, workers will demand more family-friendly employment policies and practices. In the face of these drivers, organisations will have no choice but to blur the distinction between the way they manage permanent staff and freelance consultants.

Re-structuring organisations to fit the freelance model

CASE STUDY

Dominic Shales, joint founder and head of Paratus Communications, London

Dominic Shales has seen the future of the freelance model, and in his experience it works very effectively.

After spending a good part of their twenties and thirties working their way up to senior positions in conventional PR agencies, Dominic and his partner John Rivett broke out and set up the first agency in the UK that only uses freelance consultants as an innovative way to deliver better client service. That was in late 2003. By its second birthday, Paratus Communications had become a case study in combining expert freelance talent with a robust web-based management hub to deliver real results.

'Initially,' says Dominic, 'reactions came in three flavours. The first was wildly passionate and supportive. The second was less enthusiastic, more wait-and-see. The third was completely dismissive. There are still a lot of clients who need the reassurance of an agency with a brass plate outside an office. It's their comfort-blanket.

'The most enthusiastic supporters were often those with an agency background themselves and experience of using freelance consultants. They understood the cost and value benefits that come from having low overheads and a lean infrastructure. They also knew that freelance consultants bring high levels of specialist skill and experience.'

Despite support for this new agency concept, Paratus Communications got off to a relatively slow start. The tipping point came once Dominic and John had convinced a critical mass of credible clients that their model delivered on its promise. 'We always knew it could work,' says Dominic. 'What we needed was the client list to prove it. Having the blue-chips on board has helped to generate positive coverage and more interest. Success breeds success.'

The Paratus pitch has a compelling simplicity. Instead of taking an existing team and imposing it on a client in the hope of achieving the right fit for the brief in hand, Dominic and John select bespoke teams to match the client brief from a database of vetted specialists held by its partner, freelance resourcing agency Xchangeteam. The result involves no square pegs in round holes but passionate and talented people who fit together – and fit the brief. Or as Dominic says: 'We give clients the right team, not the team that happens to be available. We act like commissioning editors – strong, strategic management at the centre, with excellent teams of people delivering the programmes for clients.'

When it comes to managing systems and workflow, Dominic acknowledges that five years ago the Paratus model would have been difficult to sustain, and 10 years ago it would have been impossible. 'The Internet may have enabled the idea of an agency like Paratus, but broadband has been critical to making the idea a reality,' he says.

Having established *why* organisations must adapt to the freelance phenomenon, it is equally important to consider *how* they should set about it. Much has been written on which organisational structure best supports the freelance model. The debate has spawned a proliferation of terms such as 'virtual corporations', 'network organisation', 'boundary-less businesses', 'team-based divisions', 'modular' or 'cellular corporation', and 'process-based' or 'horizontal organisations' – to name just a few.

Semantics aside, it is clear that any organisation planning to embed a freelance-friendly mindset must first create a structure that decentralises decision-making to teams, business units and individuals through a combination of appropriate technology, negotiation and patience. Delegation is especially important among large multinational businesses operating in complex and diverse fields. Among other advantages, delegation empowers local management to structure the working environments according to local conditions. In other words, it gives them the freedom to act like freelance consultants within the framework of a supportive corporate model.

As long ago as 1989, Charles Handy proposed the concept of the 'shamrock' organisation compromising one-third core staff, one-third sub-contractors and one-third part-timers and professional advisers. In *The Elephant and the Flea* (Hutchinson, 2001), he progresses this argument by suggesting that organisations should move towards a federation, network or matrix structure.

This solution allows organisations to expand or contract according to market conditions while achieving a balance between central control and delegation. It also gives organisations the flexibility that is essential to combining creativity with efficiency and the conflicting demands of turning a profit while operating as responsible corporate citizens.

The rise of the human factor

Future trends – **Mentors go Dutch**

Mentors are likely to play an increasingly important role in keeping freelance consultants motivated throughout an assignment. In Holland it is common practice to provide interim managers with mentoring support. In the UK, more and more of the interim management agencies are now playing a mentoring role. This is all part of a trend that places the human factor at the centre of workplace culture.

In the future, emerging technology will support highly automated processes that deliver sophisticated products and services to a market that is increasingly demanding and discerning. Rather than ticking boxes or shifting them, employees will be expected to work harder and smarter while drawing more heavily on their interpersonal skills.

Emotionally literate people who work well in teams will become highly sought after because, in future, their personal qualities will become the source of competitive advantage. Employees will be expected to develop the high levels of emotional intelligence that distinguish successful freelance consultants. As well as showing awareness, empathy and self-confidence, they will need to demonstrate flexibility and negotiating skills alongside their professional skills.

In a business environment where the human factor is such a powerful driver, organisations will need to offer employees coaching, mentoring and training courses to develop interpersonal skills that can help to enrich relationships with colleagues as well as customers.

FINALLY: DOES THE FUTURE OF FREELANCING LIE IN OUR PAST?

Some argue that human beings are instinctively programmed to follow the freelance model because it is part of our evolutionary inheritance. In his book *Managing the Human Animal in the Information Age* (Crown, 2001), Nigel Nicholson claims that we are hardwired by our prehistoric ancestors to behave in certain ways. In his neo-Darwinian view, the ideal human organisation would have small units with a flexible hierarchy and leadership. Its members would work primarily in self-regulating teams that recognise and reward individual achievements. Teams would combine diversity with high levels of trust and involvement.

If this argument is true, the freelance model is woven into our DNA – and its future lies in our past.

Key point summary

- The forces of globalisation are blurring the distinction between permanent employees and freelance consultants.

- The rise of the freelance model is accelerated by irreversible demographic drivers.

- The future belongs to those organisations with the vision and skill to treat *all* staff as freelance consultants.

- This involves embedding a supportive management culture that focuses on results, values teamworking and respects the human factor.

- To thrive, a freelance-friendly mindset requires a flat organisational structure that decentralises decision-making.

- Ultimately, argue the Darwinists, following the freelance model is part of our evolutionary inheritance.

Appendix 1

Below is a recommended master contract template for use by clients when they contract directly with a freelance consultant's company.

The template for the master contract remains the copyright of the Professional Contractors Group (www.pcg.org.uk), the representative body for the UK's freelance small business community. Neither the PCG nor the author of this book makes any guarantee as to the effectiveness of this contract in a court of law.

Master Consultancy Services Agreement

This Master Consultancy Services Agreement is made between:

A   [*Freelancer consultant's company name*] a company incorporated in [*England and Wales*] (registration number [*number*]) of which the registered office and trading address is [*address*] ('the Consultancy'), and

B   [*Client company name*] a company incorporated in [*England and Wales*] (registration number [*number*]) of which the registered office and trading address is [*address*] ('the Client').

The Consultancy agrees to supply and the Client agrees to engage the Consultancy's Services on the following terms:

1. Nature of this Agreement

1.1.   This is a Master Agreement, and defines the terms under which the Consultancy will undertake such Services for the Client as may be agreed between the parties from time to time.

1.2.   Entering this Agreement does not of itself oblige the Consultancy to provide or the Client to accept or pay for any particular consultancy services. Where it is agreed between the parties that any Services are to be provided, a schedule in the form annexed to this Agreement setting out the nature of the Services, the charging basis, and any other material terms (a 'Schedule') will be produced by the Consultancy and provided to the Client.

1.3.   On receipt of a Schedule

1.3.1. if the Client accepts its terms the Client will promptly sign and return one copy to the Consultancy

1.3.2. if the Client does not accept its terms the Client will promptly advise the Consultancy.

1.4. Upon a Schedule being signed by both parties, it will become a contract binding on the parties.

1.5. A contract formed on the basis of a Schedule referencing these terms is governed only by these terms and by no others, except where both parties expressly agree in writing. In particular, it is agreed that any Purchase Order or other such document from the Client is intended for the Client's own administrative purposes only, and that notwithstanding its wording, neither a Purchase Order nor its content will have any legal effect. Save to the extent expressly provided, all conditions, warranties or other terms implied by statute or common law are hereby excluded to the fullest extent permitted by law.

1.6. Either party may request change to the nature or scope of Services covered by a Schedule. Any such request shall be sufficiently detailed to enable the other party to assess the impact of the proposed change. No such change will become effective until agreed in writing between the parties.

1.7. This Agreement is not exclusive; the Consultancy is and remains at liberty to also provide services to third parties, and the Client is and remains at liberty to engage services (including similar services) from third parties. The Consultancy reserves the right to decline to provide any advice and assistance outside the scope of the Services as specified in Schedules agreed between the parties, even if the Consultancy may previously have provided such additional advice and assistance.

2. Services

2.1. The Consultancy will provide Services as agreed from time to time in Schedules, so far as is reasonably practicable within any agreed timescale, and with all proper skill and care.

2.2. As an independent professional, the Consultancy will not be subject to direction or control, and itself accepts the responsibility for the proper provision of Services. It is the Consultancy's responsibility to maintain adequate Professional Indemnity, Employer's Liability, and Public Liability insurance.

2.3. The Consultancy is responsible for maintaining reasonable continuity in personnel providing Services on its behalf, but reserves the right in its sole discretion to make changes from time to time; no additional charge will be made for any handover period, and the Consultancy remains responsible for Services performed by any individual on its behalf. Where the Consultancy's charges are on a time and materials basis, or where any individual who will provide Services is named in a Schedule, it is the Consultancy's responsibility to ensure that the relevant skills and experience of any replacement personnel remain commensurate with the fee rates charged.

2.4. It is the Client's responsibility to afford the Consultancy with such access and staff cooperation as the Consultancy may reasonably require for the proper performance of any Services.

3. Copyright and Intellectual Property Rights

3.1. 'Deliverable' means a work produced by the Consultancy in the course of Services for delivery to the Client. Where pre-existing works are incorporated in any Deliverable, the Client has non-exclusive irrevocable world-wide royalty-free licence to use modify and distribute such pre-existing works, but only as part of the Deliverable; all other rights in the pre-existing works are reserved. Subject thereto, all rights in any Deliverable pass to the Client upon payment of all fees due to the Consultancy which relate to that Deliverable, and the Consultancy will execute a formal assignment thereof on request by the Client.

3.2. The Consultancy will indemnify the Client against infringement of third party rights by a Deliverable, provided that the Client notifies the Consultancy of any relevant third party rights promptly on such rights becoming known to or suspected by the Client.

4. Charges and Payment

4.1. Estimates are subject to change if based on incorrect information provided by the Client, or if any specified dependencies/facilities are not available on time, or if any equipment required to be provided by the Client fails to operate correctly (save where the engagement itself is for the repair thereof).

4.2. All sums due shall be invoiced and paid as specified in the applicable Schedule. The Client will pay the Consultancy's invoices within 30 days, plus VAT. Unless otherwise specified, where payment is on a time and materials basis, the Consultancy may invoice monthly.

4.3. If payment of any of the Consultancy's invoices becomes overdue, the Consultancy may suspend provision of Services, and any agreed timescale will be automatically extended; the Consultancy may also terminate this Agreement and any current Schedule for material breach while any payment is more than seven days overdue.

5. Liability

The Consultancy is not liable for any loss or damage in excess of the higher of (a) £100,000, and (b) 125 per cent of the total sums payable under a Schedule, except where it may not lawfully exclude or limit liability. Each party expressly excludes liability for consequential loss or damage, loss of profit, business, revenue, goodwill or anticipated savings. Any liability or remedy for innocent or negligent misrepresentation is expressly excluded. Neither party excludes or limits liability for death or personal injury.

6. Termination

6.1. Either party may terminate this Agreement at any time when there is no current Schedule, by immediate written notice.

6.2. Either party may terminate this Agreement and any current Schedule at any time if the other is in material breach or if the other becomes insolvent, by immediate written notice.

6.3. Any rights or obligations of a continuing nature shall survive termination.

7. Force Majeure

If either party is obstructed in performing any of its obligations under a Schedule by an event outside its reasonable control, then performance to the extent obstructed is suspended for so long as the obstruction continues. While performance is suspended and has been so for more than seven days, either party may terminate the Schedule by immediate written notice.

8. Staff obligations and third party rights

8.1. Each party solely retains all the responsibilities and rights of an employer towards and in relation to its own employees. Neither party seconds its employees to the other. Each party will indemnify the other against any claims brought by or in relation to its own employees, whether such claims relate to employment, tax, National Insurance, or otherwise.

8.2. Neither party will employ, engage, or otherwise solicit any person who during the previous six months was an employee or subcontractor of the other and with whom such party had material contact in connection with Services performed under any Schedule, until six months after that Schedule has terminated.

8.3. No third party rights are intended to be conferred or created by this Agreement or any Schedule.

9. Confidentiality

Unless the parties have signed a separate agreement containing more specific provisions in relation to confidentiality (in which case the provisions of such agreement will continue to apply in lieu of this clause), each party will keep any confidential information disclosed by the other secret. Neither party may use or take advantage of any such confidential information without the discloser's consent, even after the end of this Agreement. This obligation does not apply to (i) information known to the receiver before disclosure by the other party, or (ii) information which becomes public knowledge without fault on the part of the receiver, or (iii) disclosures made to the extent required by some applicable legal or regulatory requirement.

10. Notices

Any notice to be given by either party to the other shall be in writing and may be sent by recorded delivery to the address of the other and shall be deemed to be served two days following the date of posting.

11. Law

These terms are governed by the laws of England and Wales, the courts of which shall have sole jurisdiction in relation to all matters arising.

Signed by the parties' authorised representatives as follows:

On behalf of **the Consultancy** by [   ]

(Authorised Signature)

Title: ....   Date: ....

On behalf of **the Client** by [   ]

(Authorised Signature)

Title: ....   Date: ....

Schedule

Schedule No. [   ]

to the Master Consultancy Agreement between
[*Freelance consultant's company name*] ('Consultancy') and [*client company name*] ('Client') dated [*date of Master Agreement*] (the 'Master Agreement')

1. Introductory

1.1. The general nature of the Client's business is [*general description, eg 'banking', 'telecommunications', etc*], and the Client requires expert assistance in connection with a project for [*general description of overall project of which the Services will form part, and project name if available*].

1.2. The Consultancy's field of expertise includes [*general statement of relevant core field of expertise*], and the Consultancy has agreed to provide the following Services to the Client, under the terms of the Master Agreement.

2. Services

2.1. [define]

2.2. [identify any Deliverables]

2.3. [specify any acceptance criteria]

2.4. [specify any dependencies]

2.5. [specify any facilities to be provided by the Client]

2.6. The Consultancy is responsible for providing its own reference materials, administrative support, and equipment [for use when Services are provided other than at the Client's own premises] [for analysis and development, and technical tools and developer libraries as necessary] [other than where use of the Client's equipment is required for reasons of security, is particularly specialised, or where the Client's equipment is itself the object of the Services].

2.7. [specify any equipment to be provided by the Client]

2.8. The Consultancy will liaise as necessary with [*name*].

2.9. The Consultancy shall be responsible for correcting any defective Services at its own cost, provided that such works are notified to the Consultancy by the Client [one month] after the Services are otherwise complete.

2.10. Any further specific details, prioritisation, and time estimates for each piece of work will be as agreed between the Consultancy and the Client from time to time. Progress reports will be provided as and when reasonably required.

3. Timetable

3.1. Provision of the Services is expected to commence on [   ] and to be completed by [   ].

Begin options

OPTION A – TIME AND MATERIALS

4. Charging basis

4.1. The Consultancy will invoice monthly for the Services on a 'time and materials' basis at the rate of £[   ] per [hour][day][, together with materials and expenses at cost].

4.1.1. Travel [other than between the Consultancy's offices and the Client's premises at [*location*] takes place during normal service hours.

4.1.2. For the avoidance of doubt there is no obligation on the Client to require Services on any particular day, and no obligation to make payment in respect of any periods during which the Services are not required, or during which the Services are not in fact provided.

4.2. *OPTIONAL – SCOPE OF EXPENSES* The Services will normally be provided on the Client's or the Supplier's premises and the Supplier shall charge no additional amount for travelling to and from these premises. In the event that the Services require the Supplier to travel to another site, the Client shall reimburse the Supplier against invoice for all reasonable expenses of and in connection with such travel, on the following basis:

4.2.1. All air travel shall be Economy Class flights

4.2.2. All rail travel shall be Second Class Rail

4.2.3. Car journeys shall be charged at the rate of £[ ] per mile plus parking fees.

4.2.4. Hotels bills, including breakfast and dinner, shall be redeemable up to a maximum of £[ ] per night.

4.2.5. A fixed additional charge of £[ ] per night will be made for each night necessarily spent overseas.

4.3. *OPTIONAL CAP FOR FEES* The total fees for the Services are capped at and will not exceed £[ ].

4.4. *OPTIONAL ESTIMATE OF CHARGEABLE TIME* The Consultancy estimates the total chargeable time required to perform the Services at [ ] [hours][days], and agrees that it will promptly seek confirmation from the Client if this estimate is likely to be exceeded by [25] per cent.

4.5. *OPTIONAL ESTIMATE OF MATERIALS AND EXPENSES* The Consultancy estimates the total cost of materials and expenses to be incurred in the performance of the Services at £[ ], and agrees that it will promptly seek confirmation from the Client if this estimate is likely to be exceeded by [25] per cent.

5. Termination for convenience

5.1. *ALTERNATIVE A1* The Consultancy may give the Client [one month]'s notice in writing to terminate the Services to be provided under this Schedule.

5.2. *ALTERNATIVE A2* The Consultancy may not prematurely terminate the Services to be provided under this Schedule, other than for cause.

5.3. The Client may terminate the Services to be provided under this Schedule immediately by written notice to the Consultancy at any time.

OPTION B – FIXED PRICE

6. Charging basis

6.1. The Consultancy will provide the Services for the Fixed Price of £[ ]. The Fixed Price may be invoiced [*on completion, or in stages – if in stages then specify when (by date, or clearly identifiable milestone) and how much for each stage*].

6.2. *OPTIONAL – SCOPE OF EXPENSES* The Services will normally be provided on the Client's or the Supplier's premises and the Supplier shall charge no additional amount for travelling to and from these premises. In the event that the Services require the Supplier to travel to another site, the Client in addition to the Fixed Price shall reimburse the Supplier against invoice for all reasonable expenses and in connection with such travel, on the following basis:

6.2.1. All air travel shall be Economy Class flights

6.2.2. All rail travel shall be Second Class Rail

6.2.3. Car journeys shall be charged at the rate of £[ ] per mile plus parking fees.

6.2.4. Hotels bills, including breakfast and dinner, shall be redeemable up to a maximum of £[   ] per night.

6.2.5. A fixed additional charge of £[   ] per night will be made for each night necessarily spent overseas.

6.3. If this Schedule is terminated prematurely, the Client will pay the Consultancy for Services provided prior to termination on a *quantum meruit* basis.

7. Termination for convenience

7.1. *ALTERNATIVE B1* The Consultancy may give the Client [one month]'s notice in writing to terminate the Services provided under this Schedule.

7.2. *ALTERNATIVE B2* The Consultancy may not prematurely terminate the Services provided under this Schedule, other than for cause.

7.3. *ALTERNATIVE C1* The Client may terminate the Services provided under this Schedule immediately by written notice to the Consultancy at any time.

7.4. *ALTERNATIVE C2* The Client may give the Consultancy [one month]'s notice in writing to terminate the Services provided under this Schedule.

7.5. *ALTERNATIVE C3* The Client may not prematurely terminate the Services provided under this Schedule, other than for cause.

End options

8. Generally

8.1. The Services will be performed under the terms of the Master Agreement, which together with this Schedule and any other documents expressly referred to in the Master Agreement or in this Schedule constitute the entire understanding between the parties relating to the subject matter of this engagement. Any earlier agreement between the parties relating to the subject matter of this Schedule is hereby superseded and is discharged by mutual consent. No other terms or changes will apply unless in writing and signed by both parties.

8.2. Neither party enters the agreement constituted by this Schedule and the Master Agreement on the basis of or relying on any representation, warranty or other provision not expressly stated herein.

8.3. This Schedule shall prevail if there is any conflict between it and the Master Agreement.

Signed by the parties' authorised representatives as follows:

On behalf of **the Consultancy** by [   ]

(Authorised Signature)

Title: ....   Date: ....

On behalf of **the Client** by [   ]

(Authorised Signature)

Title: ....   Date: ....

Notes (not forming part of the document)

1. General

1.1.   This Master Consultancy Services Agreement has been commissioned by PCG and drafted by Egos Ltd. for the use of PCG members only. It is intended to be suitable for use by a range of businesses, and in a variety of situations. While more substantial than the Terms of Business, it remains the case that compromises have been made to ensure a broad range of usefulness, and also to keep it relatively short.

1.2.   As a result, it inevitably has limitations, and there are inevitably many situations for which it will not only be unsuitable, but in which its use could be positively dangerous, whether from commercial or IR 35 viewpoints.

1.3.   Neither PCG nor Egos Ltd can accept responsibility for the use of this standard agreement in any particular situation, and it is therefore the member's *sole* responsibility to satisfy him/herself that it (including any amendments) is wholly suitable for the member's particular proposed use – if in doubt, seek advice!

2. Suitability

2.1.   This document comprises a Master Consultancy Services Agreement, and is intended to provide a suitable legal background/framework for self-contained consultancy and other service-focused tasks, when accompanied by a suitably worded Schedule.

2.2.   This agreement will NOT generally be suitable for

     2.2.1.   software development to a pre-agreed specification for a fixed price (this would generally require more specialised and focused provisions covering beta- and acceptance-testing, warranty, procedures for amendment of specification, warranty, support, and other areas)

     2.2.2.   arrangements which include the sale/hire of goods/software

     2.2.3.   provision of a specified individual for unspecified tasks

     2.2.4.   anything else which cannot be clearly/unambiguously defined in words as a *statement of specific services*

in respect of each of which other considerations (which are not covered by these terms – and are not intended to be so covered) assume a more dominant level of importance.

3. Terminology

3.1. 'the Consultancy' can be globally replaced with an abbreviated name for the Consultancy.

4. Substitution

4.1. The areas normally covered by a substitution clause are in clause 2.3 of the terms. However, since the starting point here is that this Agreement does not envisage a commitment to provide the services utilising any particular named individual, the Client is not given any express rights to approve a substitute.

4.2. If, when negotiating a contact, a Client is concerned about not having such rights, the issue can often be resolved by reminding the Client of its rights to terminate without cause and without notice as provided by the Schedule (generally included as part of the IR 35 strategy – see below).

4.3. If the commercial position requires you to concede further on this point, then you may consider adding the following to the end of 2.3:

> 'Services will not be provided utilising any individual who the Client reasonably considers lacks the necessary skills, qualifications or experience.'

5. Law and Jurisdiction

5.1. Change as appropriate – permissible jurisdictions are:

    5.1.1. England and Wales

    5.1.2. Scotland

    5.1.3. Northern Ireland

    5.1.4. the Isle of Man

    5.1.5. the Island of Jersey

    5.1.6. the States of Guernsey

6. Schedules

6.1. The areas to be covered by a Schedule will generally include

    6.1.1. Services definition – This section is not cast in stone, but is simply intended as a prompt list to assist in formulating a clear and adequate description of what is to be done as a statement of specified services. This may be freely modified as appropriate, taking care to express clearly and unambiguously, and to make the boundaries clear. The end result should suit the intended reality, and include any constraints and other task-relevant variables. Particular care needs to be taken in defining the scope and its boundaries clearly where the payment basis is to be 'fixed price'.

    6.1.2. Correction of defective services: whether or not this provision is appropriate will depend on the nature of the services. This must primarily be a decision taken on commercial grounds. Where it is commercially appropriate and included, it will generally be a significant IR 35 plus.

6.1.3. Timetable – estimate start and finish; if there is any particular period when services will not be provided (and particularly where the expectation is for services daily), then the point should be covered here, eg to make any necessary provision for holidays, etc.

6.1.4. Note that no express provision is made for time off for holidays, etc; there are primarily two reasons for this:

6.1.4.1. such a provision will often be inconsistent with an agreement to provide specific services; and

6.1.4.2. such a provision might be considered to undermine the provisions for substitution (clause 2.3).

Members should bear in mind that if they do plan to take time away from a contract and do not intend to exercise rights to substitute, then it may be wise to ensure that they keep the Client informed, and that any known dates are expressly excluded from the timetable clause in the Schedule.

6.1.5. Charging basis, and any constraints on charges. Optional sections are included to provide either for 'time and materials', or 'fixed price'; Members should note in particular the following points:

6.1.6. Where payment is on a time and materials basis:

6.1.6.1. a proper IR 35 strategy to minimise any suggestions that there is MOO (Mutuality of Obligation) will generally require (i) that the contract makes clear that there is no obligation on the Client to require Services on any particular day, and no obligation to make payment in respect of any periods during which the Services are not required, or during which the Services are not in fact provided; and (ii) that the *Client* should have the right to terminate without cause and without notice

6.1.6.2. whether the *Consultancy* has a right to terminate other than for cause will generally be a purely commercial matter, for agreement between the parties.

6.1.7. Where payment is on a fixed price basis (ie the Consultancy contracts to provide some form of pre-specified result or deliverable for a predetermined price),

6.1.7.1. MOO will generally be less of a concern

6.1.7.2. the Client is less likely to regard it as commercially acceptable for the Consultancy to have the right to terminate prematurely, other than for cause.

6.1.8. No specific provision for interest on late payments is included; this is intentional – the general provisions of the Late Payment of Commercial Debts (Interest) Act 1998 (see http://www.egos.co.uk/faq/debt_interest.htm) apply where a contract makes no reasonable provision for interest, and are more valuable than contract terms generally acceptable to a Client.

6.1.9. Any other terms specific only to this particular Schedule – insert an additional term for any that cannot be fitted into one of the above.

6.2. It is advised that the last clause remain unchanged. Note that the this last clause includes a provision that the content of this document will override any conflicting provision in the Terms.

7. General

7.1. Sections marked as **OPTION A, OPTION B** (ie all between **BEGIN OPTIONS** and **END OPTIONS**)

7.1.1. First, choose whichever section (**OPTION A** or **OPTION B**) is appropriate, and delete the entire other section. Then consider any *OPTIONAL* and *ALTERNATIVE* clauses in the retained section.

7.2. Clauses marked as *OPTIONAL*:

7.2.1. Each such clause is optional and may be retained if applicable, or deleted.

7.3. Clauses marked as *ALTERNATIVE*:

7.3.1. Sets of Alternatives are marked.

7.3.2. Only one clause from within each set of Alternatives should be chosen and retained, and the other(s) from that set deleted.

7.4. As a final check after completing the draft (and before submitting it to a Client for approval):

7.4.1. ensure that the capitalised words have been removed.

7.4.2. search for the 'open square brackets' symbol '[' to ensure that all placemarkers have been completed and all appropriate variables selected.

7.4.3. delete this final 'notes' section.

Appendix 2

Below are two recommended master contract templates:

- one for use by clients when they contract with a freelance resourcing agency, and
- one for use by an agency when contracting with its freelance consultant's company [service provider].

The template for the master contract remains the copyright of the Professional Contractors Group (www.pcg.org.uk), the representative body for the UK's freelance small business community. Neither the PCG nor the author of this book makes any guarantee as to the effectiveness of this contract in a court of law.

Agency Contract with Client

for the Supply of Services by a Service Provider

This Agreement is made the [*date*]

BETWEEN

A [*Agency company name*] a company incorporated in [England and Wales] (registration number [*number*]) of [*address*] ('the Agency'), and

B [*Client company name*] a company incorporated in [England and Wales] (registration number [*number*]) of [*address*] ('the Client').

AGREEMENT

The Agency agrees to supply and the Client agrees to engage the Services specified in the Schedule referenced [*reference*], to be provided by the Service Provider named therein, and on the basis of the Agency's Terms of Business (Agency-Client) for the supply of Services by a Service Provider (as attached).

The Charge Rate for this engagement is _[n] per [*hour/professional day (7–10 hours)*]] plus VAT as applicable, payable within [*30*] days of [weekly/monthly] invoice.

SIGNING PROVISIONS

On behalf of **the Agency** by [   ]

(Authorised Signature)

Title: .... Date: ....

On behalf of **the Client** by [   ]

(Authorised Signature)

Title: .... Date: ....

Terms of Business (Agency-Client)

for the supply of Services by a Service Provider

1. Definitions and Preliminary

1.1. 'Contract' means a contract between the Agency and the Client for specific services to be performed by a Service Provider, and comprising (in order of priority) a Schedule, any other document expressly referred to therein, and these Terms. A Contract referencing these terms is governed only by these terms and by no others, except where both parties expressly agree in writing. All changes must be agreed in writing.

1.2. Unless otherwise clear from the context, references to 'Client' (other than where contractual obligations are imposed) include any named End-Client.

1.3. 'EAA' means the Employment Agencies Act 1973, and 'Employment Agency' and 'Employment Business' have the meanings defined by the EAA. 'Conduct Regulations' means the Conduct of Employment Agencies and Employment businesses Regulations 2003. 'Opted Out' means agreement made between Service Provider and a person to be engaged on the Services, notified to the Agency, and having the effect that the Conduct Regulations do not apply in relation to an introduction or engagement.

1.4. These terms govern introductions which may be made by the Agency of independent professionals to the Client, with a view to engagements through the Agency for the performance of specified services. These terms also govern engagements for such services. By entering discussions with a person introduced by the Agency, or by allowing the commencement of services, the Client accepts these Terms.

1.5. Any Contract is conditional on the Agency contracting unconditionally with the Service Provider for the Services.

2. Service Provider Responsibilities

2.1. The Services will be provided by the Service Provider as specified in the Schedule, with reasonable skill and care, and so far as is reasonably practicable within any agreed timescale.

2.2. The Service Provider is a professional, answerable for key milestones and for deliverables, and responsible for exercising initiative as to the delivery of the Services. A Contract does not give the Client the right or power to direct or control the daily activities of the Service Provider or any person engaged on the Services. The Service Provider is responsible for:

2.2.1. maintaining adequate Professional Indemnity, Employer's Liability, and Public Liability insurance of at least the Required Insurance Cover, and for providing evidence thereof on request

2.2.2. providing its own reference materials, administrative support, and equipment where required (other than where use of the Client's equipment is required for reasons of security, because it is specialised, or because the Client's equipment is itself the object of the Services)

2.2.3. devising appropriate working strategies and providing the Services independently, in a professional manner, with all proper skill and care, and in accordance with accepted professional standards methodologies and guidelines, and with all notified specifications and procedural requirements for the Project

2.2.4. rectifying any defective Services at its own cost, provided they are notified within the Defect Warranty Period

2.2.5. maintaining and providing any necessary qualifications, authorisations, and training

2.2.6. complying with all notified IT, telecommunications, security, and Health and Safety policies, and with any other relevant legislative requirements

2.2.7. giving the Client reasonable notice of any periods when Services will not be provided

2.2.8. taking and being accountable for all appropriate decisions in relation to all aspects of the performance of the Services.

2.3. Where a Schedule names any personnel who are to provide the Services, the Service Provider is responsible for maintaining reasonable continuity, but reserves the right under its contract with the Agency to substitute other personnel of equivalent expertise. The Client has the right to refuse to accept Services from substitute personnel on reasonable grounds related to security, qualifications or expertise. No additional charge will be made for any handover period, and the Service Provider remains responsible for Services performed on its behalf.

3. Client Responsibilities

3.1. The Client has no responsibility for the Service Provider or any person engaged on the Services, other than (a) as specifically provided for under a Contract, and (b) such responsibilities as are generally owed to the public at large.

3.2. The Client is responsible for:

3.2.1. giving the Service Provider such cooperation and access as are reasonably necessary for the proper performance of the Services

3.2.2. informing the Service Provider if on any day the Services are not required.

3.2.3. ensuring that all relevant Health & Safety policies are disclosed to the Service Provider.

4. Copyright and Intellectual Property Rights

4.1. 'Deliverable' means a work produced by the Service Provider in the course of Services for delivery to the Client. It is the Service Provider's responsibility to clarify with the Client whether in the interests of saving time and cost any pre-existing works are to be used in the production of any Deliverable. Where pre-existing works are incorporated in any Deliverable, the Client has non-exclusive irrevocable world-wide royalty-free licence to use modify and distribute such pre-existing works, but only as part of the Deliverable; all other rights in the pre-existing works are reserved. Subject thereto, all rights in any Deliverable will pass to the Client, and it is the Service Provider's responsibility to provide a formal assignment thereof on request by the Client.

4.2. It is the Service Provider's responsibility to indemnify the Client against liability as a result of alleged infringement of third party rights by a Deliverable, provided the Client notifies the Service Provider of any relevant third party rights promptly on such rights becoming known to or suspected by the Client.

5. Confidentiality

Each party will keep any confidential information disclosed by the other secret. Neither party may use or take advantage of any such confidential information without the discloser's consent, even after the end of this Agreement. This obligation does not apply to (i) information known to the receiver before disclosure by the other party, or (ii) information which becomes public knowledge without fault on the part of the receiver, or (iii) disclosures made to the extent required by some applicable legal or regulatory requirement. It is the Service Provider's responsibility to provide any reasonable confidentiality agreement required by the Client.

6. Charges and Payment

6.1. Where the Schedule shows Service Reports are required, a Client authorised representative must authorise by signing (or electronically, where such procedures have been agreed) Service Reports every Invoicing Period. If the Client has any cause for dissatisfaction with performance of the Services it must note the relevant Service Report accordingly, and promptly provide any requested further details. The Agency may invoice on the basis of authorised Service Reports.

6.2. The Agency may suspend provision of Services while any payment is overdue, and while more than seven days overdue may also terminate for material breach.

7. Termination

7.1. A Contract may be terminated

    7.1.1. by either party giving the other written notice of the Notice Period specified in the Schedule.

    7.1.2. by the Client by Immediate Notice, if the Service Provider fails to provide the Services in accordance with these terms, provided the Client gives full written details and such further cooperation as the Agency reasonably requires; the Client acknowledges that such right to terminate is the Client's sole remedy against the Agency for any such failure, without prejudice to any rights it may have against the Service Provider.

    7.1.3. by either party by Immediate Notice, if the other is in material breach of contract, or is in breach of contract and fails to remedy the breach within fourteen days of being required in writing to do so, or if the other becomes insolvent or ceases to carry on business, or if any preliminary step is taken towards the other's liquidation winding up receivership or administration (other than for *bona fide* reconstruction or amalgamation).

    7.1.4. by the Agency by Immediate Notice, if the contract under which the Agency has engaged the Service Provider's services terminates (for whatever reason), or if in the Agency's reasonable opinion it is under a legal obligation to terminate.

7.2. Immediate Notice means notice to terminate with immediate effect, and shall be effective however communicated, provided confirmed in writing as soon as reasonably practicable.

7.3. Any rights or obligations of a continuing nature shall survive termination.

8. Liability

8.1. The Agency will take reasonable care in selection for any particular engagement, and the Agency has no reason to believe any information presented to the Client to be untrue. The parties agree that the Client's own knowledge of its requirements is greater, and that it is therefore the Client's sole responsibility to satisfy itself as to skills and suitability of the Service Provider. By allowing the commencement of services the Client acknowledges that it has satisfied itself as to such skills and suitability.

8.2. The Client acknowledges and agrees that the Service Provider is engaged to perform the Services as specified in the Schedule as an independent professional, and that neither the Service Provider nor any person engaged on the provision of services are under the control of the Agency; and therefore that the Agency is not itself liable for any acts defaults or omissions of the Service Provider or any such person whilst performing the Services.

8.3. Neither party enters a Contract on the basis of or relying on any representation, warranty or other provision except as expressly provided in writing, and all other terms implied by statute or common law are excluded so far as legally permitted. Liability or remedy for innocent or negligent misrepresentation is excluded.

8.4. Liability is neither limited nor excluded for death or personal injury, or otherwise where it would be unlawful to do so. Subject thereto,

8.4.1. liability is excluded for consequential loss or damage of any kind or for loss of profit, business, revenue, goodwill or anticipated savings

8.4.2. the total liability of the Service Provider and any person providing Services on its behalf in respect of a risk required by a Contract to be insured is limited to the amount of the Required Insurance Cover in respect of that risk

8.4.3. these limitation and exclusion provisions shall operate for the benefit of all potentially liable persons.

9. Employment Obligations and Third Party Rights

9.1. The relationship governed by a Contract is neither that of agent-principal, nor that of employer-employee; no person providing Services will be the employee of the Client.

9.2. The Agency will keep the Client indemnified (a) in respect of any legitimate claim or demand made by the proper authorities for all taxes, national insurance or social security contributions, in respect of payments made for the services performed by the Service Provider, and (b) against any claims that may be made by any person providing Services under employment-related legislation, unless the Client has sought to exercise the rights of an employer towards such person.

9.3. The terms of the Agency's contract with the Service Provider expressly provide for the Client (but not an End-Client) to have the benefit of the Service Provider's commitments therein and (where appropriate) to take legal action directly against the Service Provider. Any agreement between the Agency and the Service Provider to rescind or vary a Contract in a way which affects the Client's rights is therefore conditional on the Client's consent.

10. Protection of Agency's Business

10.1. Where an introduction or engagement is Employment Business and not 'Opted Out',

10.1.1. if the Service Provider agrees, the Client may before the end of the Relevant Period (a) engage from the Agency on the terms offered the services of a Service Provider who has not yet provided Services; and (b) re-engage from the Agency on the same terms as hitherto a Service Provider who has provided Services

10.1.2. the Client will not during the Relevant Period engage (a) a Service Provider (or any person who has provided Services on its behalf), or (b) any person who has been introduced by the Agency, other than under a contract with the Agency

10.1.3. 'Relevant Period' means 14 weeks following introduction, where there has been no engagement; otherwise, the longer of (a) the period until 14 weeks after the First Date, and (b) the period until eight weeks after the Last Date ('First' and 'Last' meaning the dates services were first and last provided by the Service Provider under a Contract but, in the case of the First Date, disregarding any period before any interruption of more than 42 days in the provision of Services).

10.2. Otherwise, the Client will not during a Contract or within six months following the later of introduction or the end of the most recent Contract engage a Service Provider (or any person introduced or who has provided Services on its behalf), other than under a contract with the Agency.

10.3. An introduction is deemed made on the Agency providing the Client with sufficient information for the Client to identify the person introduced, unless the Client already has a connection with such person and so informs the Agency within seven days, and (if requested) provides documentary evidence.

11. General

11.1. *Force majeure:* If a party is obstructed in performing any of its obligations by an event outside its reasonable control, then performance to the extent obstructed is suspended for so long as the obstruction continues. When performance has been suspended for more than seven days, either party may terminate the Contract by immediate written notice.

11.2. *Waiver:* Failure to enforce any of these terms is not a waiver of a party's rights and shall not prejudice its rights to take action in respect of the same or any later breach.

11.3. *Severability:* Any part of a Term which is wholly or partially void, invalid, or unenforceable shall be severed from the remainder (which remains enforceable).

11.4. *Notices:* Any notice to be given by either party to the other shall be in writing, may be sent by recorded delivery, and shall be deemed served two days after posting.

11.5. *Law:* These terms are governed by the laws of England and Wales, the courts of which shall have sole jurisdiction in relation to all matters arising.

Notes

to Terms of Business (Agency-Client) for the supply of Services by a Service Provider

(These Notes do not form part of a Contract, but should be given to the Client with the terms on first accepting instructions, in a case which might fall within the EAA and the Conduct Regulations)

If the services are to be provided under the control of the client, an introduction or engagement from an agency for services to be provided by a third party service provider may be 'Employment Business' and therefore governed by the Employment Agencies Act 1973 and regulations made under that Act.

An introduction or engagement for the performance of specified services by an independent professional who accepts responsibility for their performance would therefore generally be expected to fall outside the scope of the Act and regulations.

Where the Act and regulations apply:

1. It is the Agency's responsibility to provide a copy of its terms of business before providing its own services to the Client, and to inform the Client that:

    1.1. The Agency's capacity will be that of an Employment Business; its terms of business for acting as an Employment Agency are available on request.

    1.2. Any person providing services will be engaged under a contract for services, unless otherwise advised.

    1.3. The Agency's fees are to be negotiated; no refunds or rebates are applicable.

    1.4. If any person providing services is unsatisfactory, the Client should terminate the Contract, and advise if alternative arrangements are requested.

2. It is the Client's responsibility to give the Agency sufficient information to enable selection of a suitable person to perform the services, including

    2.1. the nature of any required services

    2.2. details of any necessary experience, training, qualifications and authorisations

    2.3. any applicable constraints on working location and times

    2.4. the start date and likely duration

    2.5. any expenses payable

    2.6. details of any known health and safety risks, and of the steps taken to prevent or control such risks

    2.7. disclosing whether any engagement would involve working with or caring for or attending any person under the age of 18, or who by reason of age, infirmity or any other circumstances is in need of care or attention.

3. A service provider which is a company and any person who is to provide services on its behalf may 'opt out' of the regulations by jointly notifying the agency, before introduction or provision of services to a client.

Agency Contract with Service Provider

for the Supply of Services to a Client

This Agreement is made the [*date*]

BETWEEN

A   [*Agency company name*] a company incorporated in [England and Wales] (registration number [*number*]) of [*address*] ('the Agency'), and

B   [*Service Provider company name*] a company incorporated in [England and Wales] (registration number [*number*]) of [*address*] ('the Service Provider).

AGREEMENT

The Agency agrees to engage and the Service Provider agrees to provide the Services specified in the Schedule referenced [*reference*], to the Client named therein, and on the basis of the Agency's Terms of Business (Agency-Service Provider) for the supply of Services to a Client (as attached).

The Charge Rate for this engagement is £[*n*] per [*hour/professional day (7–10 hours)*] plus VAT as applicable, payable within [*30*] days of [weekly/monthly] invoice.

SIGNING PROVISIONS

On behalf of **the Agency** by [   ] (Authorised Signature)   Title: ....   Date: ....

On behalf of **the Service Provider** by [   ] (Authorised Signature)   Title: ....   Date: ....

Terms of Business (Agency-Service Provider)

for the supply of Services to a Client

1. Definitions and Preliminary

1.1. 'Contract' means a contract between the Agency and the Service Provider for specific services to be performed for a Client, and comprising (in order of priority) a Schedule, any other document expressly referred to therein, and these Terms. A Contract referencing these terms is governed only by these terms and by no others, except where both parties expressly agree in writing. All changes must be agreed in writing.

1.2. Unless otherwise clear from the context, references to 'Client' include any named End-Client.

1.3. 'EAA' means the Employment Agencies Act 1973, and 'Employment Agency' and 'Employment Business' have the meanings defined by the EAA. 'Conduct Regulations' means the Conduct of Employment Agencies and Employment businesses Regulations 2003. 'Opted Out' means agreement made between Service Provider and a person to be engaged on the Services, notified to the Agency, and having the effect that the Conduct Regulations do not apply in relation to an introduction or engagement.

1.4. These terms govern introductions which may be made by the Agency of potential Clients to the Service Provider, with a view to engagements through the Agency for the performance of specified services for them. These terms also govern engagements for such services. By entering discussions with a potential Client introduced by the Agency, or by commencing services, the Service Provider accepts these Terms.

1.5. Any Contract is conditional on the Agency's contracting unconditionally with the Client for the Services.

2. Service Provider Responsibilities

2.1. The Services will be provided for the Client as specified in the Schedule, with reasonable skill and care, and so far as is reasonably practicable within any agreed timescale.

2.2. The Service Provider is a professional, answerable for key milestones and for deliverables, and responsible for exercising initiative as to the delivery of the Services. A Contract does not give the Client the right or power to direct or control the daily activities of the Service Provider or any person engaged on the Services. The Service Provider is responsible for:

2.2.1. maintaining adequate Professional Indemnity, Employer's Liability, and Public Liability insurance of at least the Required Insurance Cover, and for providing evidence thereof on request

2.2.2. providing its own reference materials, administrative support, and equipment where required (other than where use of the Client's equipment is required for reasons of security, because it is specialised, or because the Client's equipment is itself the object of the Services)

2.2.3. devising appropriate working strategies and providing the Services independently, in a professional manner, with all proper skill and care, and in accordance with accepted professional standards methodologies and guidelines, and with all notified specifications and procedural requirements for the Project

2.2.4. rectifying any defective Services at its own cost, provided they are notified within the Defect Warranty Period

2.2.5. maintaining and providing any necessary qualifications, authorisations, and training

2.2.6. complying with all notified IT, telecommunications, security, and Health and Safety policies, and with any other relevant legislative requirements

2.2.7. giving the Client reasonable notice of any periods when Services will not be provided

2.2.8. taking and being accountable for all appropriate decisions in relation to all aspects of the performance of the Services.

2.3. Where a Schedule names any personnel who are to provide the Services, the Service Provider is responsible for maintaining reasonable continuity, but reserves the right to substitute other personnel of equivalent expertise. The Service Provider acknowledges that the Client has the right, under its contract with the Agency, to refuse to accept Services from substitute personnel on reasonable grounds related to security, qualifications or expertise. No additional charge will be made for any handover period, and the Service Provider remains responsible for Services performed on its behalf.

3. Client Responsibilities

3.1. Neither the Agency nor the Client has responsibility for the Service Provider or any person engaged on the Services, other than (a) as specifically provided for under a Contract, and (b) such responsibilities as are generally owed to the public at large.

3.2. The Client is responsible for:

3.2.1. giving the Service Provider such cooperation and access as are reasonably necessary for the proper performance of the Services

3.2.2. informing the Service Provider if on any day the Services are not required

3.2.3. ensuring that all relevant health and safety policies are disclosed to the Service Provider.

4. Copyright and Intellectual Property Rights

4.1. 'Deliverable' means a work produced by the Service Provider in the course of

Services for delivery to the Client. It is the Service Provider's responsibility to clarify with the Client whether in the interests of saving time and cost any pre-existing works are to be used in the production of any Deliverable. Where pre-existing works are incorporated in any Deliverable, the Service Provider grants the Client non-exclusive irrevocable world-wide royalty-free licence to use modify and distribute such pre-existing works, but only as part of the Deliverable; all other rights in the pre-existing works are reserved. Subject thereto, all rights in any Deliverable will pass to the Client, and the Service Provider will provide a formal assignment thereof on request by the Client.

4.2. It is the Service Provider's responsibility to indemnify the Client and the Agency against liability as a result of alleged infringement of third party rights by a Deliverable, provided the Client notifies the Service Provider of any relevant third party rights promptly on such rights becoming known to or suspected by the Client.

5. Confidentiality

Each party will keep any confidential information disclosed by the other or by the Client secret. Neither party may use or take advantage of any such confidential information without the discloser's consent, even after the end of this Agreement. This obligation does not apply to (i) information known to the receiver before disclosure by the other party, or (ii) information which becomes public knowledge without fault on the part of the receiver, or (iii) disclosures made to the extent required by some applicable legal or regulatory requirement. It is the Service Provider's responsibility to provide any reasonable confidentiality agreement required by the Client.

6. Charges and Payment

6.1. The Service Provider will invoice and the Agency will pay for Services provided in accordance with a Contract, subject (where the Schedule shows Service Reports are required) to production of Service Reports approved electronically or in writing by authorised representatives of Service Provider and Client (or, if there is no Service Report, such other evidence as may reasonably be required of the proper performance of the Services).

6.2. For the avoidance of doubt the Agency is under no obligation to make payment

6.2.1. in respect of any periods during which Services have not been provided (including days on which the Client has no requirement for the Services), for whatever reason; or

6.2.2. in respect of Services with which the Client has reasonable grounds for dissatisfaction,

provided that if the Contract is Employment Business and the Consultant's status is Not Opted Out, then the Agency will not withhold payment in respect of any time actually spent providing Services and which does not exceed the Budgetary Limits.

7. Termination

7.1. A Contract may be terminated

    7.1.1. by either party giving the other written notice of the Notice Period specified in the Schedule.

    7.1.2. by the Agency by Immediate Notice, if the Service Provider fails to provide the Services in accordance with these terms.

    7.1.3. by either party by Immediate Notice, if the other is in material breach of contract, or is in breach of contract and fails to remedy the breach within fourteen days of being required in writing to do so, or if the other becomes insolvent or ceases to carry on business, or if any preliminary step is taken towards the other's liquidation winding up receivership or administration (other than for *bona fide* reconstruction or amalgamation).

    7.1.4. by the Agency by Immediate Notice, if the contract under which the Agency provides the Service Provider's services to the Client terminates (for whatever reason), or if in the Agency's reasonable opinion it is under a legal obligation to terminate.

7.2. Immediate Notice means notice to terminate with immediate effect, and shall be effective however communicated, provided confirmed in writing as soon as reasonably practicable.

7.3. Any rights or obligations of a continuing nature shall survive termination.

8. Liability

8.1. The Service Provider is engaged to perform the Services as specified in the Schedule as an independent professional, and neither the Service Provider nor any person engaged on the provision of services are under the control of the Agency or the Client; and therefore the Service Provider accepts responsibility for any acts defaults or omissions of itself and of any such person whilst performing the Services.

8.2. Neither party enters a Contract on the basis of or relying on any representation, warranty or other provision except as expressly provided in writing, and all other terms implied by statute or common law are excluded so far as legally permitted. Liability or remedy for innocent or negligent misrepresentation is excluded.

8.3. Liability is neither limited nor excluded for death or personal injury, or otherwise where it would be unlawful to do so. Subject thereto,

    8.3.1. liability is excluded for consequential loss or damage of any kind or for loss of profit, business, revenue, goodwill or anticipated savings

    8.3.2. the total liability of the Service Provider and any person providing Services on its behalf in respect of a risk required by a Contract to be insured is limited to the amount of the Required Insurance Cover in respect of that risk

    8.3.3. these limitation and exclusion provisions shall operate for the benefit of all potentially liable persons.

9. Employment Obligations and Third Party Rights

9.1. The relationship governed by a Contract is neither that of agent-principal, nor that of employer-employee; no person providing Services will be the employee of the Client.

9.2. The Service Provider will keep the Agency and the Client indemnified (a) in respect of any legitimate claim or demand made by the proper authorities for all taxes, national insurance or social security contributions, in respect of payments made for the services performed by the Service Provider, and (b) against any claims that may be made by any person providing Services under employment-related legislation.

9.3. The terms of the Agency's contract with the Client expressly provide for the Client (but not an End-Client) to have the benefit of the Service Provider's commitments herein and (where appropriate) to take legal action directly against the Service Provider. Any agreement between the Agency and the Service Provider to rescind or vary a Contract in a way which affects the Client's rights is therefore conditional on the Client's consent.

10. Protection of Agency's Business

10.1. Unless an introduction or engagement is Employment Business and not 'Opted Out',

10.1.1. The Service Provider will not (other than under a contract with the Agency) provide services to the Client, either during a Contract, or within six months following the later of (i) introduction, and (ii) the end of the most recent Contract;

10.1.2. The Service Provider will inform the Agency immediately it becomes aware if, within 6 months following the later of (i) introduction by the Agency to the Client, and (ii) the end of the most recent Contract, the Client (other than through the Agency) makes an offer of employment or engagement direct to any person introduced or who has provided Services on the Service Provider's behalf.

10.2. An introduction is deemed made on the Agency providing the Service Provider with sufficient information for the Service Provider to identify the Client introduced, unless the Service Provider already has a connection with the Client and so informs the Agency within seven days, and (if requested) provides documentary evidence.

10.3. Subject to the above, a Contract is not exclusive, and Service Provider is remains at liberty to also provide services to third parties. It is the Service Provider's responsibility to ensure that no conflict of interest arises.

11. General

11.1. *Force majeure:* If a party is obstructed in performing any of its obligations by an event outside its reasonable control, then performance to the extent obstructed is suspended for so long as the obstruction continues. When performance has been suspended for more than seven days, either party may terminate the Contract by immediate written notice.

11.2. *Waiver:* Failure to enforce any of these terms is not a waiver of a party's rights and shall not prejudice its rights to take action in respect of the same or any later breach.

11.3. *Severability:* Any part of a Term which is wholly or partially void, invalid, or unenforceable shall be severed from the remainder (which remains enforceable).

11.4. *Notices:* Any notice to be given by either party to the other shall be in writing, may be sent by recorded delivery, and shall be deemed served two days after posting.

11.5. *Law:* These terms are governed by the laws of England and Wales, the courts of which shall have sole jurisdiction in relation to all matters arising.

Notes

to Terms of Business (Agency-Service Provider) for the supply of Services to a Client

(These Notes do not form part of a Contract, but should be given to the Service Provider with the terms on first accepting instructions, in a case which might fall within the EAA and the Conduct Regulations)

If the services are to be provided under the control of the Client, an introduction or engagement by an agency to a potential client may be 'Employment Business' and therefore governed by the Employment Agencies Act 1973 and regulations made under that Act. An introduction or engagement for specified services from an independent professional accepting responsibility for them would therefore generally be expected to fall outside the scope of the Act and regulations.

A work-seeker which is a company and any person who is to provide services on its behalf may 'opt out' of the regulations by jointly notifying the agency, before introduction or provision of services to a client. Where the Act and regulations apply, then unless such 'opt out' notice has been given:

1. An Agency must at the outset provide its terms of business, and inform the work-seeker:

    1.1. that its capacity will be that of an Employment Business

    1.2. that it will pay for services provided, whether or not it is paid by the Client

    1.3. of the type of work for which an engagement will be sought and the minimum rate of remuneration reasonably expected to be achieved (to be specified in a separate document)

    1.4. that unless otherwise agreed in the Schedule,

        1.4.1. the notice required for the work-seeker to terminate a Contract will be one month

        1.4.2. payment will be made against monthly invoice

        1.4.3. there will be no leave entitlement (paid or otherwise).

2. It is the work-seeker's responsibility in any event:

   2.1. to notify any intention to opt out before introduction or supply or services to a Client

   2.2. to give details of any current engager, to reduce risk of submission to that engager

   2.3. to confirm identity (work-seeker and any person who will provide services on its behalf) including Certificate of Incorporation and (where applicable) VAT Registration Certificate

   2.4. to confirm and maintain any experience, training, qualifications and authorisations considered necessary by a client, or required by law, by a professional body, or for the proper performance of the Services

   2.5. to ensure that any profile or *curriculum vitae* supplied accurately and completely discloses history and experience, and that references are honest and accurate

   2.6. to promptly confirm willingness to be submitted for prospective engagements

   2.7. to disclose any reason it may have at any time to believe that the work-seeker or any person who will provide services on its behalf to be unsuitable for any particular engagement

   2.8. to ensure that where a Contract may require a person who will provide services on its behalf to occupy premises away from home, it has arranged for suitable accommodation and travel

   2.9. not to accept any offered engagement if it is in any way restricted from doing so.

3. Additional requirements apply if any engagement will involve working with or caring for or attending any person under the age of 18, or who by reason of age, infirmity or any other circumstances is in need of care or attention.

Form of letter to notify Opt-Out

From [*Service Provider company name*]
   [*Service Provider address*]

To:
   [*Agency company name*]
   [*Agency address*]

[*date*]

Dear Sirs:

Re: [*Service Provider company name*] and [*individual name*] – [*Agency company name*], Conduct of Employment Agencies and Employment Business Regulations 2003

We the undersigned Service Provider and individual give notice pursuant to regulation 32 of the above Regulations that we do not wish the regulations to apply to any engagements through you.

Yours faithfully,

[*Company officer*]
        pp [*Service Provider company name*]

[*individual name*]

Index

Membership has its rewards

Join us online today as an Affiliate member and get immediate access to our member services. As a member you'll also be entitled to special discounts on our range of courses, conferences, books and training resources.

To find out more, visit www.cipd.co.uk/affiliate or call us on 020 8612 6208.

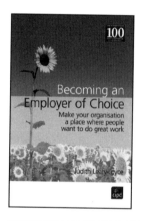

Also from CIPD Publishing . . .

Managing Performance:

Performance management in action

2nd Edition

Michael Armstrong and Angela Baron

Managing performance is a critical focus of HR activity. Well-designed strategies to recognise and improve performance and focus individual effort can have a dramatic effect on bottom-line results. The problem is to determine what the processes, tools and delivery mechanisms are that will improve performance in your organisation, as well as determine which ones are best avoided.

The authors have tracked performance management processes over the past seven years, and their comprehensive survey reveals what leading organisations are doing to manage their employees' performance and how they are delivering results.

With detailed illustrations from the real world, and clear practical advice, this text shows you how to improve the management of your employees' performance.

Managing Performance will help you:

- design performance management processes that reflect the context and nature of the organisation;
- create supportive delivery mechanisms for performance management; and
- evaluate and continuously develop performance management strategies to reflect the changing business environment.

Order your copy now online at www.cipd.co.uk/bookstore or call us on 0870 800 3366

Michael Armstrong is a Fellow of the Chartered Institute of Personnel and Development, and a Fellow of the Institute of Management Consultants. He has over 25 years experience in personnel management, including 12 as a personnel director. He has also been a management consultant for many years and is a former Chief Examiner, Employee Reward, for the CIPD. He has written a number of successful management books, including *The Job Evaluation Handbook* (1995) and *Strategic HRM* (2002), both co-written with Angela Baron; *Employee Reward* (third edition 2002); *Rewarding Teams* (2000); and *New Dimensions in Pay Management* (2001). All are published by the CIPD.

Angela Baron has been Advisor, Organisational and Resourcing at the Chartered Institute of Personnel and Development since 1990. Her other books, *The Job Evaluation Handbook* and *Strategic HRM* were both co-written with Michael Armstrong.

Published 2004	1 84398 101 7	Paperback	192 pages

The Chartered Institute of Personnel and Development is the leading publisher of books and reports for personnel and training professionals, students and all those concerned with the effective management and development of people at work.